AN ARTIST'S GUIDE TO LIVING IN DIVINE

Created
to Thrive

MATT TOMMEY

Contents

Endorsements

Creativity is going to define the next generation of what God is doing on the earth. To have tools and resources to understand identity will set people apart in industries and the art world itself. I am so glad to read Matt's book on creativity. You will find a great expanding perspective as you let the pages fill you and teach you from a man who comes across as a humble expert. I highly recommend it!

Shawn Bolz

Author of Translating God, God Secrets, Keys to Heaven's Economy
A host of Exploring the Prophetic podcast
www.bolzministries.com

I don't know anyone more diligent in helping creative people to discover, develop and effectively deploy their gifts!

Ray Hughes
Selah Ministries
www.rayhughes.org

Matt Tommey is a gifted artisan, teacher, and mentor. His book "Created to Thrive" is a great resource for anyone looking for encouragement and practical wisdom in their journey of art making as a vocation.

Stephen Roach
Musician, Poet, & Host of the *Makers and Mystics* podcast
www.makersandmystics.com

Long ago I learned that a true mentor is a person who is wise from his failures and is made humble by his successes. Two things I learned in reading Matt Tommey's book, Created to Thrive. First, had he been around 47 years ago and was older than me (impossible) his book would have saved me years and years of failure, and secondly, I would have fallen on my knees and begged him to mentor me, because he is not afraid to share his failures while humbly pointing to the promises and principles of God that make for success as a "starving artist" in the world and in the Kingdom. YEA GOD!

Papa Ken Helser
www.aplacefortheheart.org/helsers

If one is a believer and an artist or aspiring artist, this book may just become your "go to manual." Matt Tommey has produced an inspirational and practical book for all who are interested in the creative arts. Sadly, in many churches today the visual artist often feels disenfranchised and misunderstood, and in many cases doesn't know where to turn for help.

In this book, Matt Tommey will encourage, enlighten, and give a strong theological basis for the creative arts. He also provides a practical approach to idea getting, goal setting, and business strategies. His writing style is fluid and interesting, making for an easily understandable book. As a college professor of art and studio artist of 50 years, I can honestly say that this book should be required reading for every Christian artist.

Gary Wilson
Professor of Art Emeritus and Studio Artist
www.wilsonbibleart.com

In the Church, we talk a lot about God being loving, holy, omnipotent, faithful, and just. But we rarely, if ever, talk about the fact that the *first* thing God reveals about Himself in Scripture is that He is *creative*. I am so thankful that Matt is helping artists make this connection, embrace the call to create, and integrate the gospel more deeply into their work."

Jordan Raynor
Author of Called to Create: A Biblical Invitation to Create, Innovate, and Risk
www.calledtocreate.org

In "Created to Thrive," Matt Tommey issues a much-needed call for excellence in the art that Christian artists produce and that Christians purchase. Matt backs up every facet of this call with evidence from scripture and examples drawn from his own success as both an artist and a marketer of his work."

Bob Hay
Founder, Karitos Creative Arts Conference
www.karitosnation.org

Inspiring and energizing! Matt has been faithful to take the steps God gave him to thrive as an artist and person. Now he shares those proven steps with so that we, too, will learn to thrive in our creative callings.

J. Scott McElroy
Author of Creative Church Handbook and 'Finding Divine Inspiration,'
Director, New Renaissance Arts Movement
www.jscottmcelroy.com

Pat and I both are very pleased with what Matt has laid out before people in his new book - the process by which we change into what we had hoped to become. It seems that people can't seem to figure out how to change their thought processes and bad habits by simply being led to the water and urged to drink, even if it's been explained to them in detail. It has become rather like looking in the mirror, then when walking away and forgetting what you've just seen. This book lays it all out in a fashion that somehow avoids that issue; both in a simplistic and orderly manner for artists, as well as anyone else interested in getting bigger and better results with their lives.

Jim and Pat Banks
www.houseofhealingministries.org
www.traumaprayer.com

Matt Tommey is not only a gifted artist and visionary. He is a risk taker and encourager and mentor, always willing to share the wisdom he has learned on his journey of faith and art. If you need encouragement or are looking for focus in your journey, get this book.

Manuel Luz
Musician & Author of *Imagine That*
www.manuelluz.wordpress.com

All throughout history God has raised up fathers to be a voice to the sons and daughters of their generation. I believe Matt Tommey is a father to many spiritual artists in this generation that are about to rise up and thrive in the creative arts across the world. Matt's words have inspired me to believe what I thought I couldn't believe and they have called me to create from my true identity as a child of God. You will walk away with courage and a new outlook that will produce results as these words are applied. I thank God for the Gift That "Created to Thrive" is.

Aeron Brown
Artist & Musician
www.aeronbrown.com

If you are an artist, know an artist or want to be an artist, then

Matt Tommy's "Created to Thrive" is a book you will run to again and again. Matt is a champion for all of us who desire to thrive as artists. You will find keys that help you to identify roadblocks, overcome disappointments and position your life for successes. Matt is bold, honest and wise in his writing and this book will not disappoint. "Created to Thrive" is perfect for personal motivation and group empowerment alike. It is a master class in drawing artists to excellence in ministry, artistry and the marketplace. There is no better news than this.

Vivien Hibbert
Musician, Speaker, & Author
www.vivienhibbert.com

Matt has an extraordinary gift of making the prophetic practical and simple for artists! He has proven that success is not an illusion, rehearsed hope or a daydream but an attainable reality. Best of all, he provides solid, freeing steps that any serious artist can embrace to flourish within their passion.

Theresa Harvard Johnson, M.Div.
www.schoolofthescribe.com

Matt Tommey was not content with simply being an accomplished artisan. He answered God's calling to inspire and even challenge others to explore their own creative expression. His latest book, 'Created to Thrive,' is yet another powerful tool that he provides for us. Matt shares his heart and journey that led to his place as a forerunner. I'm proud to call him a friend and greatly encouraged by all he does to promote Kingdom through the arts!

Janice VanCronkhite
Artist, Speaker, Instructor, & Mentor
www.jvcartworks.com

Scripturally-based, inspired and inspirational, thought-provoking and challenging, *'Created to Thrive'* is a 'must-read' for every artist seeking a breakthrough, the next step and/or success as a thriving artist. Master craftsman, musician, author and mentor Matt Tomme shares his wealth of experience and encouraging testimonies from the uncomfortable journey artists and artisans can face, shining a welcome light, beacon of hope and guiding star on the creative's path. Packed with wisdom and creative insight, this book tackles the nitty-gritty stuff and as you co-labor with the Holy Spirit, navigates you back on course with your divine destiny. Wonderfully uplifting and powerfully practical!

Bhari Long
Prophetic Artist and Author of ARTISTS & ARTISANS AWAKE!
www.propheticartists.com

In *Created to Thrive*, Matt Tommey's heart for God and artists comes alive. Through authentic stories, practical examples and Spirit-inspired insights, Matt leads artists on a journey for cultivating their life and art. A must-read for every artist who's thirsty to thrive and pursue their creative calling with abandon.

Joey O'Connor
Grove Center for Arts & Media
www.thegrovecenter.org

Matt Tommey's passion for Christ and his dedication to the arts shines on every page of his fourth book 'Created to Thrive.' As you read Matt's stories and revelations, the concept of choosing to thrive as a creative Christian will unfold. You'll be commissioned to run with focus and power toward a clear vision, and embracing each chapter will establish a "new normal" in your thinking as a musician, artist and/or writer in God's new Renaissance. Matt gives you practical and spiritual tools for becoming the gatekeeper and gardener of your renewed mind. Let the 'army of artists' flourish!

Wendy Manzo
Founder, Prophetic Art Australia, and Author of *The Prophetic Artist* and *88 Days*
www.wendymanzo.com

WOW!!! I found CREATED to THRIVE to be so very much more than simply a 'good read,' although it is indeed that as well. The text seemed to explode into different portions of my Being like flying Truth 'bullets'.

With the Power Enlightenment of the True Spirited Prophetic, Matt seemed like a spirit superhero. As he wielded his pen like a light ray gun, he blasted down enemy lie strongmen at the same time pulling my creative heart into the Intensive Truth Care it needed.

This Kingdom Reality/Truth painted with an artist perspective brings hard-hitting resurrection empowerment for our Creative Being. It is all there; transparency, humor, empathy, testimonies, and equipping. Matt tells the truth about where he was and now is with previews of where he is headed. He bids us follow along. Not follow him as much but rather to take his lead and follow the Lord together. He gives us the priceless and insightful warning that creative expression, leading or not leading to success, can be deadly if not sourced and maintained by a relationship with The Creator.

I love his Master Gardener understanding about seed life and the maturation necessary for true fruitfulness. As a Worshipper, his heart understanding and dependency on intimacy tutors us in the how to know (yada) and truly honor and glorify the Lord through a life lived out in fulfillment of the Creator's design.

I found Matt, a true Friend; of the Lord and to all of us who hunger and hesitate in our hearts deepest desires. Matt preached, prophesied, encouraged, as well as kicked our butts where needed in his passionate desire to get us fully running the race the Lord has placed before each one us.

In my eyes, this is not a book for only a certain people group. It is, as I believe Matt intended it to be, a Syllabus and guiding light in Creative Kingdom Living for all of Father's sons and daughters. Because of our Father's Creative DNA within us, we are all designed to create with Him for His glory. Thank you, Matt, for shining the Light on His pathway for us.

Christine Potter
Moravian Falls, NC
www.potterhausmusic.net

It is an honor for me to endorse this roadmap for success Matt Tommey has written, to help us all navigate our way to living the fullness of the abundant life Lord Jesus paid the ultimate price to give us. I believe God will use this book to so expose the enemy of creativity, lurking in the shadows, whose sole purpose is to steal our dreams, kill every ounce of creativity within us, destroy all hope, and make us prisoners of poverty, living in the hopelessness of darkness and despair; constantly running a race like rats on a wheel. Thank You, Father, for using this wonderful, chain breaking book, to break old mindsets and patterns of thinking, opening doors and windows, and fresh winds of revelation and understanding in the hearts and minds of everyone who reads it. Thank You, for explosions of Holy knowing, and every artist hearing, this is the way, walk therein; hearing Your voice like they have never heard it before! Thank You, Father, for using this book to help launch and empower the army of Sons of Light into this Kingdom Renaissance that is upon us; making them healthy, wealthy, and wise.

James Nesbit
Artist, Author & Speaker
www.jnesbit.com

Matt Tommey balances spiritual inspiration, practical advice, and personal storytelling for unlocking godly creativity. As a Christian artist, I can truly say that *Created to Thrive* resonates, and I encourage anyone interested in leading a creative *and* Spirit-led life to read this book and apply his concepts. His words are clearly God inspired to breathe fruitfulness into anyone who reads it!

Janet Hyun
Artist
www.janethyun.com

I have known Matt for six years and have witnessed his authentic way to live his faith-inspired career as an artist, entrepreneur and as a father to the artistic community worldwide. This book is a must-read for anyone pursuing a successful career as an artist but also for those who are still dreaming about it but also appeals to people who wish to create out of intimacy with God for their own personal journey.

Matt is not only talking about the process of growing in your artisan calling. He invites us to be sons and daughters and to pursue a real relationship with Him in order to live in our true identity as children of God.

This book will provide you with tools to thrive artistically in order to bring transformation in today's society.

Mayra Pankow
Artist, Speaker & Instructor
www.mayrapankow.de

Created to Thrive" will help take you from a frustrated artist with "no time or money," to what Matt describes as a "thriving artist," with an abundance mindset and a fruitful creative ministry.

Whatever creative endeavor the Lord has placed on your heart, whether in church ministry or creative business endeavors, you will find within this book inspiration and practical strategy to move into the destiny God has for you.

Don't believe the lie that to follow the creative calling on your life means you will need to always be struggling financially! God has revealed strategies, tools, and keys to release you into an abundant and provisional destiny that will not only be a joy to fulfill but will also bless many. Matt covers this in a way that is easy to digest with a big dose of encouragement on every page.

Roma Waterman
Award Winning Singer/Songwriter, Author, & Speaker/Trainer
www.romawaterman.com

Introduction

For most of my life, I had no clue what it meant to actually thrive in life. I was a Christian, I loved Jesus, I was creative, but I had no clue what it meant to actually live an abundant life in God's Kingdom, much less thrive in my finances, creativity, relationships, and other parts of life. Somewhere along the way, things changed for me big time, and my life was fundamentally transformed.

In fact, it's been so transformed that I would say it's been as powerful an experience for me as was my initial salvation experience. See, when I received Jesus into my heart, I was made new. The challenge was, I had no idea how to walk new, think new, and live life in that new reality. Once the Holy Spirit began to show me how to cooperate with Him based on my divine design and His leading, all of a sudden, life completely changed.

The biggest revelation I had on this journey was understanding the fact that thriving in my life and my creative design was not just some sort of feel-good, self-help psychobabble, but rather, it was God's express design for my life. You got it; this was His idea from the beginning. It was God's idea to create me with a specific design that would glorify Him, allow me to experience abundant life, provide for my every need, enable me to hear His voice in the context of an intimate relationship with Him, and be used by Him to release His nature in the earth. Sure, God used the difficult things in life to teach me and bring me into maturity, but His overwhelming desire is that you and I live in the fullness of His very best. As the song says, "You're a good, good father, It's who you are. And I'm loved by you. It's who I am..."[1]

My desire for you is that through this book, you'll be able to enter into a new reality that you are deeply loved by the Father, that He has good plans for you; to prosper you, to give you a hope and a future, that all you have to do is begin to align with His reality and experience true abundant life. Let's jump in.

Matt Tommey
www.MattTommeyMentoring.com

---

[1] *©2014. WorshipTogether.com / sixsteps Music / Vamos Publishing / Housefire Sounds (ASCAP).*

A New Way of Living

*I have come that they may have life,
and have it to the full.* John 10:10 NIV

I'm not really the poster child for what most people would call a typical starving artist. I've written four books for artists that have sold thousands of copies and gone all over the world. I'm a speaker and have spoken to thousands of artists throughout America and in really cool places like Australia, Scotland, Germany, England, and even Spain. I'm also a professional artist in Asheville, North Carolina where I create nature-inspired woven sculpture for luxury mountain and coastal homes, and because of that, I've been featured in countless print and online publications.

Now, it might sound a little weird, but I've always had this passion to both create my artwork and to help other artists thrive. I especially help them break out of that all too familiar starving artist mentality and step into the fullness of who God created them to be as an artist. But you want to know something really interesting? Just a few short years ago, I too was a frustrated, starving artist. It's true.

I was 36 years old, and we had almost lost everything. The economy was starting to tank during the beginnings of the Great Recession, and things were really rough. Two years earlier, I had a successful marketing company, and then three of my biggest clients went bankrupt. Cash was tight, and bills were piling up. Add to that my mounting frustration of having built a company I was no longer creatively energized by and it was a recipe for major stress.

I eventually closed the company and got a job for a major technology firm doing inside sales and marketing. Now picture this, me, a creative entrepreneur and artist now forced to work in a cubicle for eight hours a day. It was literally hell. And on top of that, after being there only 11 months, I was laid off due to the growing recession.

There I was with no job, no company, very little money, and a whole lot of unfulfilled dreams, especially ones around my own art and creativity. I felt completely defeated, confused, frustrated, and left wondering, "Where is God in the middle of this mess?" I was truly running on empty. Somewhere along the way, I had lost the real me. I had just about given up on myself, my creativity, the dream of my own business, and even God.

Then one day, almost by accident, everything changed. I remember it like it was yesterday. I was sitting in a parking lot having just turned down a job at a huge church when I blurted out something like, "Well God, what am I gonna do now?" Just as quickly, he responded to me saying, "Matt, don't look for a job, your provision is going to come like popcorn. Go home, lay on the floor and worship me."

Well, I'll be honest. I didn't understand, but I did it. Literally, for the next six to eight weeks, that's exactly what I did, and during that time, my entire inner GPS system was recalibrated. I started to find the real me again. Music and creativity started to flow. A passion for natural materials and making my baskets returned, and money started flowing into my life through jobs that supernaturally came my way. I also had a series of dreams that confirmed my life calling as a father to artists and even had someone give me a building so I could start to raise up an army of artists. It was as if I had stepped out of the desert into an oasis of blessing.

At first, I kept wondering, is this for real? Then I realized it was not only real, but it was my new normal as an artist in the Kingdom of God. Once that started to sink in, everything changed. As time went on, I realized this was much more than just a goose-bump filled spiritual high. I was getting powerful strategies from the Holy Spirit about marketing, business, creating with God, my identity, and how all these things fit together in my life as an artist. It's almost like I stumbled upon some ancient pattern that artists had been searching for over the centuries and yet, these truths had always been there, covered up the whole time.

I had discovered a simple pattern for thriving as an artist that was life-giving and profitable, creatively energizing and centered in my relationship with God. I couldn't believe it. My life changed overnight.

I call it double doors of favor, and it was almost embarrassing. Opportunities were abundant, creative inspiration was flowing, money was no longer a struggle, and everything started converging beautifully. Listen, I know this can all sound a little too good to be true, but all I ask is you hold off from disbelieving long enough to see the evidence for yourself.

Over the next six years, I kept practicing what I was learning and kept growing in every area, thriving the whole time. My sculptural basketry work started flourishing so much I went full time and opened a studio in Asheville's River Artist District. My work started growing in popularity and selling for thousands of dollars, so much so that I had to hire people to help me.

I was writing books like *Unlocking the Heart of the Artist,* and suddenly, they were going around the world. I was being invited to speak and hosting artist conferences myself like the Gathering of Artisans to help artists start to connect with God, create, and step into their dreams. It was amazing. I felt like I was living the dream.

At first, I didn't want to share all this because it almost felt like bragging. But then I did. I started sharing these simple strategies with other artists, and you know what happened? They started thriving too. It was incredible!

I had discovered a different way of living for artists that was literally changing lives forever, and it was way beyond just knowing the hottest new marketing trends. People were starting to align with their divine design, and it was like turning on a water spigot of strategy, provision, and divine inspiration. The best part? I was full of peace, creatively fulfilled, close to God, happy at home, and making a six-figure income from creating my art. Sounds almost crazy, doesn't it? Sometimes I still have a hard time believing this is real.

Hope is Not A Strategy

Here's something that you might have never heard at church before. Hope is not a strategy for changing your life. No matter how hard you pray, God's not going just to come down and zap everything to make it all better. Most people, especially in church, are taught to come to Jesus, go to church, follow the rules, and don't screw up. If you manage to do all this, then at the right time God will bless you because He knows best, almost like Santa Claus.

The reality is, that's not how the Kingdom works, and it causes something I call Mailbox Mentality. You pray, pray, pray then hope, hope, hope, and every now and then you walk out to your proverbial mailbox to see if God brought you anything according to your wishes. It's a quick recipe for depression and frustration, and it definitely doesn't honor God.

If you grew up like I did, you probably have some issues with being creative, especially as a vocation. Believe me; I didn't just have a few issues; I had a lifetime subscription. I believed all the lies most artists believed like, "Artists don't make money," or "You need to get a real job," or "You'll never be as good as that person, so you might as well not try." How about the one that says, "Art is a frivolous pursuit. It's time to grow up because you have real responsibilities."

The truth is, most people believe this stuff, and no matter how much they try not to believe it, it's like a movie that plays over and over in their heads. It affects how you live your life, what you believe is possible, and even how you see God. Trust me; it's a no-win situation. In that way of living, being a starving artist is just about the best you can hope for.

Every artist I've ever spoken to has dealt with or is dealing with major identity issues surrounding this idea of being able to thrive and really step into the fullness of who God has called him to be as an artist in His Kingdom. This has been the main challenge in my own life as well.

In my first book, *Unlocking the Heart of the Artist*, I shared openly how the identity issues I struggled with as a young man hindered me as I tried to navigate life and ministry. I wanted to build a successful and prosperous life for myself and my family, but all I had to work with was a really broken blueprint for my life. The Bible says in John 10:10 that "The thief comes only to steal and kill and destroy; I have come that they may have life, and have it to the full." (NIV) You see, the enemy used events from my life and an unhealthy paradigm to do major damage in my life. It wasn't until I started really renewing my mind to what God's truth was about my life that things started to change.

Learning how to step into who God says you are and how to receive all that He has already provided for is really one of the major things—if not THE major thing—that you as a creative person have got to get. Otherwise, you'll just sit there loaded with all these incredible gifts that God has invested in you and not able to step into the fullness of expressing those things.

and church

There's another belief that you might have picked up from other artists, it goes something like, "Just believe that life is hard, that being an artist is difficult, that you can't sell your work without selling out, and that if you're an artist, you're doomed to suffer." That's one of the most prevalent beliefs out there among artists, and it's just another recipe for depression and frustration.

The bottom line is that you have two choices in life. You can choose to do what everybody else is doing, believe the same lies that everyone else believes, and you'll achieve the same limited outcome you always have. Or you can realize that there's a better way, one that leads to that full life Jesus told us about. That's what I did. I realized there was a different way to live and be creative based on how God designed His Kingdom to work. I learned that, and if I plugged myself into His system of life and creativity, my life would change in phenomenal ways.

After years of walking in this new way of thinking as an artist, I finally discovered a pattern for artists that will revolutionize the way they think, create and experience life. I know, because that's what it's done in my life. The best thing about this blueprint is that it works for anyone, at any time, in any place in the world, because it's based on God's Word. When you start aligning yourself with God's design for your life and your art, things are going to start changing big time!

Imagine just for a moment, life the way you have always dreamed it could be. Feeling connected to God and hearing His voice, creating with the Holy Spirit, following His lead as you share your art and see it transform people's lives. Imagine if you will, the work that you create being highly desirable and people paying hundreds or even thousands of dollars to purchase it from you.

What if you could transition out of your current job into selling your art part-time, or even full-time. Instead of being frustrated with your marketing, being able to know where to show your work, how to price and present your work to people who have the means to purchase it.

What about even connecting with other artists who value the same things you do and helping each other grow. I know it might sound like a dream, but this, my friend, is the life God has designed for each of us as artists. Believe me; it is completely realistic and possible for you. It's the life I'm living right now and the life other artists just like you are starting to experience as well.

This is why I'm so excited about this book. Everything that I'm going to teach you is the stuff I do every day, the stuff that God has worked on and is working on daily in my heart. It's the power of Kingdom, and it's working on the inside of us to bring a real transformation.

Signs & Wonders

There are two more things I want to say just as we get started. First, you know a lot of us have prayed over the years, "God, use my work as a sign and wonder, release miracles and the power of the Kingdom," and I fully believe that God wants to do that in every creative medium that we practice, so that when people look at our works of art, they will get healed, transformed, and set free! When people listen to our music, they will be set free from depression and all the things that bind them.

But even more than that I believe that God has not only designed us to create works of art that He will use as signs and wonders to demonstrate the power of the Kingdom but that He wants to do such a work in us that our lives will be a sign and wonder as well! We are literally going to interact with people, other artists, other creative people, and other people that are in our circle of influence in a way that they see the power and favor of God at work in our lives. Signs that will make them wonder and ask, "Man, I don't know what you are doing, I don't know how this is working out for you, but I've got to know, what is this all about?"

It's funny, as I'm writing this today, a friend of mine who I've known for years just showed up at my studio today asking if we could connect for coffee after a delivery he was making in Asheville. This fellow was a student of mine; he is a great artist and a guy who has his own art business down in Georgia. Of course, I said, "Okay, great."

After sitting down to a cup of coffee together, he said, "Matt, I'm making some money, but I am scared of success. I don't know what I am doing, I don't know what success looks like, I don't know what my purpose is, and it looks like you got it all together. How can I have it all together?" He continued saying that even though we don't know each other that well, "From the outside, it looks like God is really blessing you and you have an incredible thing going on. I would just love to hear your story." So, even though we weren't that close and he's not even a believer in Jesus, he saw something different in me and was bold enough to ask. He saw a "sign," and he began to "wonder." As we sat there for next hour and a half at a coffee shop, I just shared my story with him, mistakes, wrinkles, and all. When I got home, I told my wife, "This was a complete, total, divine appointment thing that happened today. Wow!"

Wherever you are in your journey today as an artist, I'm just going to believe that God is going to so transform your heart, that you are going to be a sign and wonder, not just create signs and wonders. I believe that God will not only use you to create beautiful things, but you are going to be the beautiful thing that God transforms to release His power, His glory, and His nature in and through your life. So I hope you are ready for that!

And the second thing, just by way of introduction, is this concept of choosing to thrive in your own life. This is going to be a different concept for most of you, and that's okay! Most of us have structured our lives around the positive and negative experiences we've had personally and have witnessed in the lives of others around us. We are all the product of our thoughts, feelings, and experiences as well as the good, bad, healthy, and unhealthy things that others have imparted into our lives.

What I'm asking you to do as you read this book is start living from a different blueprint, playing from a different playbook, and beginning to see your life without limits. I'm asking you to start to choose new habits, create new patterns of living, and create a life in concert with the Holy Spirit and with God's Word. I'm asking you to start establishing a new normal for yourself, a new reality that's not based on experiences, fear, anxiety, what momma said, what your friends have said, or what you've believed all these years. I want you to establish a new normal based in the Kingdom of God.

Here's the deal, no matter what you've experienced, no matter how good or bad things have been, no matter how much money you've made, no matter how good or bad the economy is, and no matter where you are in the world, the truth is the Kingdom of God is always on, always working, always active, and always available to us. You can either choose to stay plugged into the same old way of doing things that everybody else does, or you can choose to plug into the life of God's Kingdom.

It's learning to change your inner narrative that's on repeat inside your heart to one that aligns with the reality of the Kingdom of God. When you learn to do that, friend, believe me, your life will change drastically.

Without Vision

Where there is no vision, the people perish. **Proverbs 29:18 KJV**

We moved to Asheville in late 2009 on a word from the Lord that He was moving me to "a seat of influence in the art world to put me in the seat of influence." I didn't understand it all. But the Lord opened the doors, and after 13 years of being in Atlanta, we moved. At first, I was on staff at a local church leading worship while finishing my first book, *Unlocking the Heart of the Artist*, continuing my passion of working with artists and working on my hobby, at that time, of making baskets. I was happy, but because I didn't have much context for how growth in God's Kingdom happened, I found myself in perpetual waiting mode; waiting on God to do something.

The more I waited, the more frustrated I became, and then thankfully, the Lord showed me something really foundational. What I was lacking was not the movement of the Lord, but a clear vision for my life. As I read Proverbs 29:18 again and meditated on its meaning for my life, I started to understand how this thing called vision really works. The Bible says, "Where there is no vision, the people perish." (KJV)

Now, you might have been familiar with this verse for your whole life. It's one of those things you hear in church when leaders are trying to rally the troops for a new building campaign, but there's so much more to this verse! Personally, it's such a key verse because the word "vision" that is used there is much more than just simply "sight" or "seeing." The word there actually means "prophetic revelation" or "spiritual understanding." So as you read that verse again, you start understanding that without prophetic revelation, or without receiving real revelation and connection to the Holy Spirit, people perish, or more accurately, cast off restraint.

How God Releases Revelation

Let me pause here and clarify something for you in regards to prophetic revelation. When you read that phrase, you might be under the impression that all prophetic revelation happens the same way, but that's simply not the case. There are some things that the Lord will speak directly into your life that seem completely out of the clear blue sky. You weren't praying for it; you weren't asking about it, then BOOM, He just spoke. Maybe it happened while you were reading your Bible, or going through a situation in your life, or receiving a prophetic word from someone. Don't get me wrong; it's awesome when that happens! I've had many encounters like this over the years, but it's not the only way revelation happens.

The other way I see the Lord bring prophetic revelation is through our imagination. As we dream with Him, as we actively seek and envision what could be possible, He confirms His plans and reveals more than we could ever envision on our own. Both types of revelation are from God, but without understanding how the Father uses both methods, you'll be confused on how this vision thing actually works. I'll discuss all of this in more detail later.

Casting Off Restraint

When you think about somebody casting off restraint, you can almost imagine someone running willy-nilly in desperation, screaming, "Just get me out of here!" When you don't have vision in your life, you run to and fro chasing money and opportunities. You spend your life in a desperate quest trying to be successful any way you can. The whole time the Holy Spirit is saying, "Listen, if you'll just connect with me and let me download some prophetic revelation, some real understanding to your life, about what you are designed to do, and what the Kingdom is all about, you won't have to cast off restraint. It is possible to run with focus and power toward a clear vision."

It reminds me of a story from a woman in my artist mentoring program, who shared:

> *"The thing that I was missing was co-laboring with the Holy Spirit. I had compartmentalized my Christian life and my art life without even realizing it. Even though I knew that God gave me my creative gifts, it never occurred to me that they go together. Hand in hand. I also had lost my identity in Christ over the years of fighting and pushing through things on my own strength. Through Matt's mentoring program, I am learning to mesh it all together and rediscover my identity in Christ Jesus. That comes first folks. Now, I am training myself to be disciplined in my studio practice and to be balanced. I feel like I am on the very edge of a breakthrough!"* J. Freimann

After I closed my marketing business in Atlanta during the height of the recession, I really had no idea how the Kingdom worked. I did what everyone else was doing. I frantically looked for a job that would pay the bills. I did everything I could on my own to make it work. I invested in real estate, and I lost money. I sold insurance, and I made money; then I lost money, and then I ultimately quit. I even worked an inside sales job for a year cold calling corporate IT departments in small to medium-sized companies. This was not God's best for my life. One thing it did do, however, was develop a raging hunger inside of me that said, "There has to be more to life than what I'm currently experiencing!"

The Preeminence of Vision

One of my favorite leaders, Michael Hyatt, said: "Vision and strategy are both important, but there is a priority to them. Vision always comes first, always. If you have a clear vision, you will eventually attract the right strategy; if you don't have a clear vision, no strategy will save you." If you don't understand where you're headed, then having all the strategy in the world won't matter because you'll have no idea where you're going.

I've met so many people over the years just like myself who grew up in the church and tried to live on the treadmill of "pleasing God." They spent their lives trying to do what they thought was right or holy without ever asking the Holy Spirit to show them His vision for their life.

As spiritual as it might sound to live that way, in reality, it's a very frustrating place because you never know where you're heading. Instead of living out of your own God-inspired dreams, you end up trying to fulfill everyone else's vision for your life. You'll never figure out your purpose in this thing called life, and you'll never see the over-arching vision God has for you, your divine design, or even your life purpose. Every opportunity will be a struggle: "Do I say yes? Do I say no? Is this even right for me?" Without understanding your divine design in the context of God's plan for your life, you have absolutely no measuring stick by which to evaluate life's new possibilities as they present themselves.

The Holy Spirit wants to begin supernaturally downloading His vision for your life, one that is in line with how you were created, and He wants to start right now. As He does, and as you accept this, His vision will become the vivid measuring stick by which you can begin evaluating everything in your life, be it opportunities, finances, relationships, creative pursuits, or even time management.

Understanding Prophetic Revelation

This prophetic revelation that I'm talking about comes through a variety of channels. One way it comes is through God's Word. You could be reading the Bible and all of a sudden; the Holy Spirit starts speaking something incredible to you that you've never realized before. Another way is through an internal impression, like a dream, vision, or a prophetic unction. You might start to feel something, know something, or get some confirmation about a prior idea or impression you had.

Then, there are the "divine appointments," those external situations, coincidences, or chance encounters, where you see the confirmation of the things God has shown you through His Word, or the things you've felt in your heart manifested right in front of you. Regardless of what channel it comes through, revelation is always flowing. God is always speaking and revealing His nature, His will, His desires, and His plans. The question is not about whether God is speaking, but rather, are you aligned to receive?

One of the things many well-meaning people say is something

like, "Well, I'm just going to wait on the Lord. I am waiting for him to speak," as if God's up there, but He's just not speaking. See, the truth is, God is always speaking, He is always showing His nature, and He's always revealing the next thing for your life, and it's never the same way for everyone! The way He speaks to me is probably different than the way He speaks to you. God continually uses a variety of situations and methods to speak to us in order to keep us close to Him. His desire for us is to avoid the rut of thinking that God is supposed to speak in this way or that way, through only this method or that method. He wants us to cultivate a fluid relationship with Him.

Revelation not only shows you who God is, but it also shows you who you are, your assignment, what you can have, and what you can do as His son or daughter in the Kingdom. As His revelation clarifies the vision for your life, it gives you context for what it is you're designed

to do and your unique place in the Kingdom. Friend, unless you connect with that prophetic revelation, you are going to end up casting off restraint and running around like a chicken with your head cut off.

Revelation Creates Healthy Boundaries

I like to think about life as a river. A river is a powerful and beautiful thing when it's flowing in its banks. Otherwise, what you have is a flood and the potential for a really big mess. You might have a lot of water flowing through your life, but if you don't have any banks, you're probably experiencing a lot of frustration. You might think, "Gosh, I'm connected to the Father, I love Jesus, and I'm sensing all these wonderful things from the Lord, but it just feels like there's no focus, no effectiveness, like my life is just spread out everywhere." Well, the reason is lack of revelation and lack of prophetic vision, because it's that prophetic vision that forms the banks around your life so that the river of inspiration can be focused to flow with purpose and direction.

You can have tons of inspiration in your life, lots of ideas for businesses, art projects, and ways to do things in life, but again, just like Michel Hyatt says, "You know you can have all the strategy in the world but if you don't have vision it doesn't do any good." The same is true here. You can have a lot of inspiration and lots of ideas, but if you don't have direction, then you have nowhere to focus that inspiration and see it manifest in your life.

How God Births Vision

It's important to realize that God births Kingdom influence through the dreams of His people. Now, I don't know if you've ever thought about this, but a lot of Christians have what I've called Mailbox Mentality. I touched on this briefly in an earlier chapter. It's a performance-based way of living that requires you to follow the rules, to not mess anything up, and if you do life well enough, then you get to go out to the proverbial "mailbox" to see if God chose to bless you today.

If you find what you're looking for, then all is good, but if not, then all of a sudden shame, fear, control, and anxiety start flooding in. Those negative feelings only exacerbate the issue, and before long you get confused, overwhelmed, and we resort to praying and even begging God to do something, anything, to fix our situation. In the middle of these times, it's easy to use phrases that sound really spiritual like, "Oh, I'm just waiting on the Lord," but in reality, you're frustrated, not knowing where to turn or how to see your situation change.

Bill Johnson said in his book, *Dreaming with God,* "While most of the Church is waiting on next move of God, God is waiting on the next dream of His people." You see, God could do anything He wanted at any time. He could save the whole world in one moment, end poverty, heal every person, release His manifest glory all over the earth at any time. "So why doesn't He?" you might ask. Because he's chosen to release His nature, His kingdom, and ultimately, the transformation that comes as a result through His sons and daughters, regular people just like you and me.

Listen, friend; God has purposefully brought you and me into this so that as sons and daughters, we can be a part of this process with Him. This is probably a seismic shift in your thinking, but it's at the very core of what it means to thrive as an artist in the Kingdom. It's about you and me connecting with the Father, and in turn, connecting with our design in the Kingdom so that God can use us to release His transformative nature into the earth, all while we experience the abundant life Jesus promised.

Think about it. I look at my life right now and think, "Are you kidding me?" I get up every day, make art, make a fabulous living, make money selling my art, and authentically connect with the clients who love what I create. Not only that, but I have many other opportunities to share this incredible journey I'm on with artists all over the world as I travel, speak, write, encourage, and mentor others along in their journey. I mean, this is more than I could have ever dreamed of and God is like, "Matt, this is great, but I have even more for you than this, if you just keep connecting with me."

This is foundational for you to understand because everything in the Kingdom comes back to this. God transforms you, and then He awakens you to realize your identity in Him. As you start to align with this new reality, He releases transformation through you as a conduit of blessing, healing, and favor. All the while, you get to experience the abundant life He promised. It's incredible, and that experience is not just for the few, or what some like to call favor. It's called the Kingdom working normally.

Seeing with New Eyes and Hearing with New Ears

Understanding the vision for your life is also based on being able to sense with spiritual eyes. It's not just what you see when looking at the natural world or your regular understanding. It takes connection with Holy Spirit; it takes connection with your unique self so that you can begin to see, hear, sense, and feel what the Spirit of God is saying to you at any one time.

God is going to speak to you differently than he speaks to me. You and I are wired differently, and we enjoy different things. When I am inspired and hear the Holy Spirit begin to speak, I usually hear His voice in the context of my own creative voice, which for me is basketry or music. If you're a painter, dancer, musician, metal artist, or potter, you might interpret the same revelation differently than others simply because you hear through the ears you've been given. I encourage you to resist this idea that revelation only comes one way or in one style. God desires for you to hear and understand what He's revealing through the unique creative voice He's given to you.

Before you read the next chapter, check out the free resource I have for you, How to Create a Vision Board, at:

www.MattTommeyMentoring.com/cttfree

Discovering the Vision

Faith is the substance of the things hoped for, the evidence of things not seen.
Hebrews 11:1 KJV

I grew up in a pretty straight-laced evangelical home. So, the concept of God speaking to me other than through His word or vague impressions through prayer was pretty foreign to me. As I started maturing in the Lord, I started being around others who talked about clearly hearing the voice of the Lord and about prophetic giftings. I was not only excited to know that God was still speaking to people, but that He also wanted to speak to me!

Of course, along the way, I learned some lessons, and one of the big ones was how people hear the Lord differently and the challenges that can cause when not walking in maturity. I can't tell you how many church staff meetings I've sat through where someone said something like, "Well, the Lord told me XYZ," only to be met with, "Well, brother, I'm not sure I agree with that because the Lord told me ABC." I would walk out confused and frustrated. I knew both people, and I knew their heart for the Lord, but something wasn't being communicated. Usually what happened is that whoever was in power played what I call "The God Card," kind of like a spiritual ace of spades that trumps every other card, and everyone else was forced to go along with his interpretation.

Now as I've matured in the Lord and learned more about walking with others in our redemptive gifts, I realize what was happening in those meetings. God wasn't confused, we were. Rather than one person being right and one being wrong, we were just seeing different facets of the same solution interpreted through the lens of each person's design.

You see, we all receive revelation and inspiration differently, which is why the Body of Christ is so important. If anybody ever tells you, "This is what God said," you have to realize what they are communicating to you is their interpretation of what God showed them based on their unique design and lens for processing life. God might speak the same thing to you, but you'll probably hear it differently simply because of your design and life experiences. That's the beautiful, mysterious, and artful dynamic of life in the Kingdom. God speaks the same truth, but it's often wrapped in a different metaphor that speaks uniquely to you.

- 2nd Corinthians 4:18 "fix our eyes not on what is seen, but on what is unseen ." (NIV)

- 2nd Corinthians 5:7 "We walk by faith and not by sight." (NIV)
- Hebrews 11:1 "Faith is the substance of the things hoped for, the evidence of things not seen." (KJV)

Realize revelation is not based solely on the way that you see things and understand things with your natural eyes, but rather by the Spirit. The Holy Spirit wants to attune your heart and your spirit so you will be connected with Him in such a way that as He moves, breathes, and shows you things, you can respond to and move with Him in a very natural way. God wants us all to become "Naturally Supernatural." This dynamic is not just some special experience that happens when the worship gets really great at church, or when a preacher lays his hands on you. This is normal Christian life; being able to see, hear, sense, and respond to the Holy Spirit with your spiritual eyes, not just your physical understanding, and honoring that same gifting in others that are on the journey with you.

How God Releases Vision

When God reveals something to you, He might give you an impression, a sense, or a feeling. He might give you a word, a verse of scripture, or He might give you all of these things. At that moment, as you're connected with the Holy Spirit, and all of those impressions and revelations start to flow, they will eventually come together to form a picture of what God is saying. Revelation always creates a faith-filled, Spirit-led picture that lives inside of us. This picture will activate and engage your imagination in the process. This is so important, because your heart and your imagination, your internal processing engine, are designed as an incubator to manifest anything you put inside.

If you've read the Parable of the Growing Seed in Mark 4:26-29, you know Jesus tells a story where a farmer takes the seed, which He later reveals to be the Word of God, and puts it in the ground, which turns out to be the heart. Overnight and throughout the day, the ground brings forth a shoot, and it says no one knows how it happens. In other words, the process of the heart manifesting fruit is a mysterious process. When you put things in your heart, they will manifest into reality. That's a fact. Yes, your heart is designed to manifest the seeds you plant in it without regard to the fruit. Whatever seed you plant, or allow to be planted, into your heart will produce some fruit or outcome in your life. Whether the outcome is good or bad depends on the seed you sow into your life. It's just how the process works. Obviously, this has huge implications for both the life we live and the art we create!

Images and Vision

Images help your heart, or your subconscious, to emotionally connect with what you're telling it, and begin to shift towards the revelation that you've received. I believe this is how faith gets built and cultivated in your heart. Faith gets developed and strengthened as the picture on the inside of you becomes more real than the picture of what you are experiencing every day.

We'll talk about this process more as we go along, but realize that your thoughts are literally physical substances that connect with other thought substances in your brain, forming patterns and pathways that subconsciously operate about 95% of what goes on in your life. Your thoughts impact your feelings, interpretations of life, and responses to others. Your thoughts determine what risks you take and what you believe is even possible. Let's look at how these seeds implanted in your heart grow and become manifested in your life.

First, you receive some revelation or inspiration that comes from a variety of sources: art, life, relationships, and yes, even the Holy Spirit. If you entertain and welcome this revelation, it's then planted in your heart. There it begins to incubate and grow. Through this incubation process, those images and feelings begin to manifest fruit in your life. Hopefully, it's the fruit of the Kingdom that manifests in your life but again, that all depends on what you plant and how you steward the process with the Holy Spirit.

One important thing to remember is this: you don't have to welcome and receive every thought, feeling, or impression that comes to you. By relying on the Holy Spirit for guidance, you'll be able to discern or know, what's His voice and what's just static from your environment.

Cultivating these living images inside your heart is vital to thriving as an artist in God's Kingdom. They become an anchor point and an altar of remembrance you can constantly return to as life happens. These living images remind you of who God is, who you are in Him, what He's said about your life, where you are going, and what He's promised you.

Transformed to Release Transformation

Remember, this transformation is not only for your benefit, although you will benefit greatly from it as a part of God's design. It's so you can become an ambassador of transformation and a conduit for His nature to flow into the lives of those around you. Just think about this simple fact: everything in this world including this book, your computer, your smartphone, the desk you work at, along with the chair you sit in, all of those things started as a speck of inspiration in someone's mind. Everything we see around us started in somebody's imagination as a simple idea. The more people watered the inspiration, the more it grew inside of them. Over time, they began to receive strategy and tactics as relationships, skills, and resources started to converge in what seems like a beautiful, divine conspiracy.

You probably recognize this process, because it's the way creativity normally happens. I wrote extensively about this process of prophetic creativity in my third book, *Creativity According to the Kingdom*. In that book, I shared the following process:

1. **Revelation:** God reveals something to you.
2. **Agreement:** You agree with that revelation, permitting it to begin manifesting through your creative expression.
3. **Skillful Response:** You begin to respond to the revelation through your artistic skill and unique creative voice.
4. **Incarnation:** Your creative response actually comes into tangible form as inspired by the Holy Spirit.

5. **Transformation:** As God moves in, on, and through your life and creative expression, His transformative Life and Light are released.
6. **Abundance:** The fruit of transformation in God's presence.

The same process is applicable when the power of the Kingdom is released in and through your life. It doesn't just have to be artwork. You can co-create the life you desire with the Father as the Holy Spirit inspires and leads you. That's why having a divine revelation for your life is so important. Without it, you'll easily be tossed to and fro any time a new picture of what's supposedly true comes up in your mind, or a new challenging situation arises in your life, or some new difficulty comes your way.

As a son or daughter in God's Kingdom, you are designed to participate with God in the creative process as you co-create an abundant life with Him. Even in the very first part of Genesis, God invites Adam and Eve into the creative process by having them name everything, care for everything, and have dominion over everything He created. He's about involving us in the process of releasing His nature into the earth.

Look at Jesus, from the moment He started His ministry and gathered the disciples, what did He immediately do? He sent them out to do the work of ministry in His name. Even Paul talks about the role of pastors in equipping the saints for their work of ministry. Participation in God's creative process is our role, our destiny, and our inheritance as we live an abundant life in the Kingdom of God.

Often there are aspects of life you consider to be fruitless desires or things God never would or ever could use. It's always interesting when God chooses to use these very things to create the greatest impact in your life. For goodness sake, look at my own story! I was a hobbyist basket maker who loved going to the woods, collecting vines, and bringing them back to make beautiful works of art. I loved that process and guess what the Lord said to me? He said: "Matt, I am in nature, I created it, and I love you. I created you, and I love that you love the natural world. I want you to create these woven sculptures because they bring you life and joy because when you do, it brings glory to me. As you follow my lead, I am going to bring clients to you, and they are going to bless your socks off and pay more for your work than you ever thought possible. As you create, I am going to make you a sign and a wonder in the art community in your area. I am going to use that story of redemption, not only through your art, but I am going to let you share that all over the world."

Wow! That's not just God's promise, that's my actual story! It can be your story, too, if you choose to plug into this dynamic with the Holy Spirit.

As Much As You Want

I can remember one time I was frustrated because we were in a church that was continually saying things from the pulpit and in prayer meetings like, "Revival is just around the corner," "God's about to break in and do something incredible," or "If we just wait on the Lord, He'll show up and bring transformation to our community." I shared that with a spiritual mentor of mine, Pat Banks, and evidently, she started praying for me. A few days later, I saw her again, and she told me, "The Lord wants you to know that you can have as much of Him as you want, anytime you want. All you have to do is ask." At that moment, I experienced some major freedom. It was like the blinders were taken from my eyes. It can be the same for you, right now. Begin to connect with this process of receiving revelation and vision from the Lord and then walking in it. It's a wonderful process. It's how the Kingdom works.

Jesus said in Mark 11:24, "Whatever you ask for in prayer, believe that you have (already) received it, and it will be yours." (NIV) That might not seem like the normal way you pray but try it. The way most people pray goes something like this: "Oh God, things are really bad, and I really need you to show up. Would you please come and do XYZ?" They continue to pray in this pattern multiple times a day thinking that God is going to respond to their begging, when in reality, God responds to our faith. The Bible says in Hebrews 11:6, "Without faith, it is impossible to please God." (NIV) My advice to you is always pray from a place of Spirit-led vision, not flesh-induced need.

God's Word teaches us in 2nd Peter 2 that we've already received everything we need for life and godliness, and that we get to participate in the Divine Nature through His very great and precious promises so that we might escape the lusts of the world. WOW! What a powerful promise!

Now, just to clarify and speak to a concern some might have, lust is simply taking a normal desire and pointing it in the wrong direction to gratify the flesh. Knowing that you'll start to realize how lust can fuel almost any set of flesh-centered desires. It's really important that we operate in the Spirit. Otherwise, we run the risk of running out ahead of God and creating a big mess!

Remember, the Bible says the Kingdom of God already lives inside of us, so it's not a matter of God doing anything else for us, per se, but rather a matter of us receiving what God has already done and placed inside of us via His Kingdom. I can hear you saying, "Oh my gosh Matt, this is so different than anything I've ever been taught." Well listen, this is called the finished work of Jesus, and it's actually really good news. Jesus didn't just come to keep you out of hell. He came so that you and I would be restored fully into relationship with the Father, His Kingdom, and have everything He designed for us to have, in order to do everything that He has designed for us to do in this earth as His ambassadors.

Like it or not, your life up until now has been the sum total of what you have believed, the seeds you've allowed to be planted in your heart, the fruit those seeds have produced, and the habits that have been formed around that fruit. Whatever you put in your heart is going to manifest as the fruit of your life. That's just the way we're designed by our incredible Creator. It's just kind of like gravity. No matter how good or bad of a person you are, if you step off a building, you are going to fall. Why is that you ask? Because the law of gravity works, all the time. God designed your heart to work in the same way. Whether you put in bad seeds or good seeds, they are going to manifest fruit in your life. The whole point of this journey together is for you to start seeing the fruit of the Kingdom manifesting in your life, not the fruit of bad decisions, fear, or self-doubt.

Cultivating Your New Normal

Two really powerful ways you can begin to build your new inner narrative is through using Biblically based affirmations and creating a vision board. I use both in my daily life and have found them to be really effective tools the Holy Spirit uses to realign my thinking to His. In the eCourse and study guide that goes along with this book, I've given you some exercises that will help as you start developing your own scripture-based affirmations and vision board. You'll also continue to develop these tools throughout your journey as you become the person and artist that God created you to be. I can't stress enough how vital it is to God's vision for your life in front of you as you begin to align yourself with His plan. This is going to become "your new normal."

Here's a quick example from one of the artists in my mentoring group about how a vision board can be a really powerful tool in your journey to breakthrough:

"I have known I was an artist and desired to follow that career path since I was fifteen. Unfortunately, other's opinions, fear, and other decisions in life took me the long way around the

mountain. I was naturally gifted and self-taught with some professional teaching here and there. I tried going back to school for art while working a full-time job. The odds seemed to be against me as an artist until I found Matt's "Unlocking the heart of the Artist" book and the Created To Thrive Mentoring program.

It was a long-time prayer of mine to find a mentor and spiritual community that supported me and my gifts. The very first thing that was released in me was an incredible feeling of permission. Permission to be myself in the group and it was welcomed. Permission to emerge and thrive as a kingdom artist. And finally, permission to make money with my art. It was the first time in my life I felt it was "ok" to make money with my gift.

Matt has given me incredible courage to continue to believe the dream can be a reality. After a week in the Created To Thrive group, I created my vision board. This was instrumental in seeing four things come to pass within three months. I sold several pieces of art; I completed illustrations for a children's book I had written, I went from a home studio to a professional shared studio space. I now have art hanging in a gallery, and I've had my first showing. These are four things I could take off of my vision board to make room for other dreams, goals, and desires. I am so grateful that God aligned my life with Matt, without him and his Mentoring program I know my heart and my art would still be where they were 6 months ago!" D. White, SC

I'd also recommend taking inventory of the relationships you have in your life and whether or not you choose to share this journey with them. You might have relationships with people in your life that might not be supportive of your desire to change. You probably already know who they are. You want to share this journey with people who will actually support you in this process. If not, you will face a lot of frustration and discouragement and find yourself set up for failure.

If you don't have anybody right now, and I pray that you do have people like that in your life, then please reach out via Facebook to artists you're already connecting with. In fact, I have an incredible artist mentoring program online that's full of artists who are going through this same transformative process. Every day, they use our website and our Facebook group to share their journey and receive encouragement from me and each other. Whatever you do, just start pursuing healthy community with other creatives who love Jesus. You were made for community. To learn more about this amazing community of artists, visit www.MattTommeyMentoring.com and click on "Artist Mentoring." There you'll find a short video I created to introduce you to this amazing group.

Hey, you're on your way! I just released supernatural grace to you in this process of transformation as you begin to align with God's design for your life. This is exciting!

As A Man Thinks...

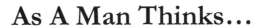

As he thinks in his heart, so is he.
Proverbs 23:7. NKJV

I can vividly remember the season when I started understanding how my thoughts created my reality. It literally changed everything about how I viewed my life and what was possible. No longer was I simply waiting for something to happen or trying to gain favor with God through obedience. I realized I had the opportunity to become an active participant with God in my own development. Yes, it was still His grace that was empowering me and His Spirit that was leading me, but I had a role to play in God's plan for my life. This was a gamechanger for me. Even though this might seem like a new concept to you, realize it's completely Biblical and grounded in how God designed us to cooperate with Him as we fulfill our unique design.

Proverbs 23:7 is one of my all-time favorite verses of scripture because it really underscores the idea that you are a product of what you repetitively think about, meditate on, and connect with emotionally. Further, when you examine the meaning behind the words, you start to realize there's a lot more being said than meets the eye. That's definitely the case here, and within several other scriptures, I'll be sharing along the way.

As we examine this short passage, I want to take it apart word by word, so you really understand what's being said. The word translated "thinks" in our Proverbs text actually means to reckon, evaluate, and act as a gatekeeper. Isn't that a great visual example? I love that because again, it positions you as sons and daughters in the Kingdom cooperating with the Father to either allow or refuse access to the thoughts and beliefs that want to enter your heart. It's telling you something really important: you are not a victim. You don't have to be at the mercy of every thought, feeling, or situation that comes your way, but rather, you can either open or close the gate to your heart at will. Now granted, that's a learned skill and a big part of what you'll be learning to do as you read this book, but understand it is possible. And, not only is it possible, it's God's design for how you steward your heart.

The second word that intrigues me is the word "heart." This isn't just referring to your physical heart, but rather the seat of your desires, emotions, passions, or appetites; in a word, it's your soul. When you put those two ideas together, you have this beautiful picture of a person being responsible as a gatekeeper for the things that are allowed in his heart. Why is this important, you might ask? Well, it's vitally important because, at the end of the verse, it simply says "...so is he." In other words, whatever you allow to be planted in the fertile soil of your heart is, over time, going to determine the fruit of what manifests in your life.

I think of it like gravity. God designed the world and established a law called gravity. It simply says under normal conditions, what goes up, must come down regardless of who you are, what you have, or even what you feel. The same is true with this law of the heart. Your heart was designed as an incredible incubator to bring forth fruit in the form of your life based on whatever seeds you put inside. You can put seeds of doubt, fear, and anxiety, or you can plant seeds of faith, love, hope, and God's Word. Either way, your heart will produce fruit.

See, it's easy to complain about your "lot in life," but when you realize that what you're experiencing is a direct result of the seeds you've sown in your life, it causes you to have, as we say in the south, a "come to Jesus meeting." Reality hits home as you start understanding that if you want to see change happen in your life, you have a role to play.

Again, this doesn't remove God from the process, but rather enables you to understand how God's design for change works in your life. Once you get hold of this and start to apply this new understanding, life becomes a huge adventure with the Holy Spirit as your guide. It's going to get even more fun as we talk about how God uses things like neuroplasticity and our brain's reticular activation system to reinforce our new normal in Him!

Just to reinforce this concept of thoughts creating the life we experience, let's take a look at two other portions of scripture. In Job 3:25, Job says of the horrible situation that has surrounded his life, "What I feared has come upon me; what I dreaded has happened to me." (NIV) Amazing isn't it? Almost like a magnet, the things that Job feared, dreaded, and meditated on in his heart came upon him and wreaked havoc in his life.

Secondly is one of my favorite portions of scripture, the Parable of the Talents in Matthew 25, which we're going to discuss in depth later in the book. I wanted to bring one part of this story to your attention as an example of a limiting mindset. In Matthew 25:24 it says, "Then the man who had received one talent came. 'Master' he said, 'I knew that you are a hard man, harvesting where you have not sown and gathering where you have not scattered seed.'" (NIV) Remember this guy in the story? He was the one who got one talent when the others received two talents and five talents and out of fear, hid it in the ground returning no profit to the master when he returned. Now, here he is with the master upon his return explaining why he couldn't show any profit based on the investment the master gave him. Do you see his reasoning? It was his belief about the master. What he believed about the master directly affected his ability to produce a return on the master's investment. That's huge! His fear-based thinking about the master being a 'hard man' literally paralyzed his ability to do the very thing for which he had been equipped and positioned.

Just take a moment right now and think about your life. Are

there things that you've believed about God, your life, your calling as an artist, or your creative talents that have literally paralyzed you from being able to move forward and thrive? Friend, listen, you don't have to live like that! The Holy Spirit is here right now to bring truth into those thoughts, shed light into your heart, and release healing so that you can start moving in a new direction!

One of my favorite quotes is from James Allen's classic book, *As a Man Thinketh*, which says,

> *"A man's mind may be likened to a garden, which may be intelligently cultivated or allowed to run wild; but whether cultivated or neglected, it must, and will, bring forth. If no useful seeds are put into it, then an abundance of useless weed seeds will fall therein, and will continue to produce their kind."*

You might be used to operating within a completely different paradigm, thinking that everything that happens to you is just by chance or because that's just the way life is. Understand, my friend, God has given you the opportunity to align with His divine design for your life, and as you do, your life will begin to bear the fruit of the Kingdom in exponential measure.

How does this happen, you might ask? Well, there are several core concepts, but let's start with agreement. The power of agreement is a core principle in the Kingdom of God. Whatever you agree with, you welcome into your life. You can agree with the lies of the enemy, your past experiences, trauma, woundedness, or difficulties, and by doing so, you continue to give them permission to operate and multiply in your life. You can also come out of agreement with those things and come into agreement with who God is, what He says about you in His Word, and by doing so, give Him permission to manifest the Kingdom in your life. It really is your choice.

This is probably new territory for you, but realize that this process is just like strengthening a muscle. The more you do it, the stronger and more agile that muscle becomes, until finally, like in golf, your muscles start to remember and begin working on autopilot.

If you're like most people, you probably have more experience with an experience-based, fear-based system of thinking than you do a God-based, Word-based, Promise-based way of thinking. That's okay. As you start cultivating the soil of your heart and planting new seeds, transformation will happen. It really is a very simple process, but one that will take your focused effort.

Your Inner Conversation

Understand that within your mind, you have a conversation going on 24 hours a day, seven days a week. It's like a movie that plays over and over again, never letting up. This "movie" is born out of and shaped by your inner paradigm. What's a paradigm? It's like your inner GPS system, and it's formed over time through repetition of thoughts and feelings. It literally controls your logic, how you spend your time and money, what you feel, your effectiveness, your willingness to take risks, and your ability to stick with it in times of challenge. Unless you alter your paradigm, no lasting change will ever happen in your life.

"But can't I just pray and ask God to come make everything different?" No, I'm afraid that's not how it works. When you got saved, the Holy Spirit came to live inside of you, and by Him, the Kingdom of God was established in your heart. It's not a matter of begging God to do anything in your life, but rather learning to align yourself with what He has already done through establishing His Kingdom inside of you.

Hopefully, you're starting to realize your thoughts literally shape your reality; not just your spiritual reality but your actual physical life experience. To push your understanding a bit further, let me share another quote from James Allen's classic book , *As a Man Thinketh*, which says:

"The outer conditions of a person's life will always be found to be harmoniously related to his inner state... (People) do not attract that which they want, but that which they are."

I also love what William P. Young, author of The Shack, says of this transformative process:

"If transformation is by the renewal of the mind and I have never changed my mind, then be assured I am actively resisting the work of the Holy Spirit in my life."

Wow! Again, whatever you believe in your heart and meditate on with regular repetition is what's going to manifest in your life. Change your thoughts, change your life.

How Your Inner Paradigm Forms

Your inner paradigm essentially comes from two places: genetics and experience. Your genetic predisposition explains why you look the same as your parents and why you have some of the same tics and personality quirks they have as well. As I look at my own life, I'm 44 right now, and some of the things that I do and say, even the mannerisms I employ, are exactly like my mom and dad. How did that happen? Well, partly genetics, but then the other side of that equation is environmental influence.

I heard somebody say if you took an infant from America and placed him in China and let him grow up there, he would immediately begin to acclimate to that environment by learning the language and adopting their customs as if he'd never even heard of America.

Erwin McManus speaks of this dynamic in his book, *The Artisan Soul*:

> "The soul is made of malleable materials. It forms itself around whatever material is forming it."

Over time, that paradigm and inner narrative begin to solidify and become what I call your normal operating procedure informing everything you do, say, and feel.

The environment in which you live and the genetics you are born with play a huge part, scientifically, in setting the stage for how you interpret life. They code you internally with a normal operating procedure regarding how to think about love, money, resources, opportunity, provision, safety, relationships, creativity, and your willingness to take risks. By the time you reached six years old, most of that normal operating procedure was hardwired inside of your heart.

Dr. Bruce Lipton, in his groundbreaking book, *The Biology of Belief: the Power of Consciousness, Matter & Miracles,* said of this process, "The first six years of a child's life, it is like a tape recorder is on. Everything it sees, smells, touches, experiences in any way, whatever it hears, is being downloaded into the brain before the consciousness of the child is even made apparent."

A Different Kind of Normal

Coming to understand these inner paradigms has been quite interesting for me as an artist who creates sculpture for luxury homes. I'm privileged to work with people who are uber-wealthy, where money and what some would see as the normal financial constraints of life are not an issue for them. They've generally got multiple millions of dollars and several multi-million-dollar homes, so it's absolutely life on a different plane. I love being around them because the Lord always uses those experiences to challenge me about my own paradigms about life, money, happiness, and what's possible.

Recently, I was visiting with a real estate developer not far from Asheville who had opened a luxury mountain home community. One of their friend's children was the realtor in the new community, and I learned that anybody who wants to buy or build a home in that community does so through them. Needless to say, they're making huge commissions, and it's a pretty sweet gig.

I remember when I got there I was impressed because this realtor was in his early to mid-twenties. I started thinking about how this kid had been set up in this incredible situation where he's selling one to five-million-dollar houses on average, making a generous commission every time one of those houses sells. Then it hit me. He probably grew up in an environment believing this was normal. He probably came out of college believing that money and opportunities come easily, that a six-figure annual salary is normal, and that he would get there very quickly in life.

Well, that normal might not be the same for somebody who's living in poverty, but it was his normal. As you ponder this, it might be easy to think, "Well, that's not fair," or, "He's privileged," or something like that. Right now, I don't want you to think about this story in terms of right or wrong, good or bad. I just want you to realize that the inner paradigm for this person was set and imprinted on them from a very early age, and now this is the normal from which he operates every day. If you want to change, you have to change your paradigm.

The Fruit of Your Life

Understand the life you're experiencing right now is a direct result of the inner paradigm that's been formed in your life. It's the fruit of the movie playing in your mind. You might have no clue that this dynamic is even working in your life. But know that as you mature in the Lord, and maybe even get sick and tired of your current circumstances, you might just realize: "Hey, I don't have to live like this anymore! I can change!"

Hopefully, that's where you are right now! Instead of being a victim of circumstances, you can start aligning with God's divine design for your life and experience all He that has for you. You can start choosing to change that inner paradigm in order to reflect what you really want and what God says about you, based on your unique design, passions, and dreams.

There's only one question that remains at this point. Will you continue to believe the lies of the enemy based on your past experiences, or will you begin to align with God's Truth? It's a simple question, but unless you're willing to move out of agreement with the past and into agreement with God's Truth, there's really no need to keep reading. Otherwise, if you don't learn to master your mind, you'll remain captured in a roller coaster of emotions, living a life you were never designed to live.

Another quote from Erwin McManus' book, *The Artisan Soul*, sums it up nicely when he says:

"Eventually, somewhere down the road in the silence of a paralyzing moment, we have to decide what voice will define us and what story we choose to be in – which is the narrative that guides."

What voice will you allow to define your future? What's it going to be? I'll give you a minute to decide...

Resistance to Change

If you're still reading, then congratulations, you've chosen wisely! As you begin this journey of recalibrating your inner GPS, there are a few more things you need to know. First, it's going to feel uncomfortable because it's new. It's like working out. The first two weeks you're sore and wondering, "Is this even working" and then all of a sudden, you begin to see a glimmer of hope. The same is true here. It might take a minute to feel some momentum start to flow, but it is on the way!

It makes me think of a story from one of the members of my artist mentoring program who shared this about shifting her paradigm:

> *"When I joined this group, I was pretty lost. I had been a moderately successful wildlife artist for almost 40 years when I moved to another location where no one knew me or my art. I didn't know how to start over, so I retired."*

After becoming a part of the mentoring program, she started seeing her paradigm shift specifically with what she thought was possible in her art sales. She started renewing her mind, setting goals and actively working with the Holy Spirit to renew her mind. Even after a couple of setbacks, she started to have marked change. Here's what she said:

"Matt put out his "90-day goal" challenge. I wrote them down and submitted them. I kept them small because I wanted to attain them. One of the goals was to sell at least two pieces of my work per month, either originals or prints. I had already sold two prints, so that goal was met for December! Less than a week later, the gallery manager called and said another customer had bought two prints and wanted to buy several more! She said he had been at a recent reception and wanted to meet me. Then she said, "Aren't you glad we sat down and changed your prices?" I am so blown away by this! I am convinced it was changing my paradigm and trusting the Lord to take care of me! I do feel like I have been set free!" J. Kimble

Secondly, you're going to discover people in your life who would prefer you to stay the way you were. Your growth might be uncomfortable for them, so you might have to make some hard decisions regarding those relationships. As you grow in this new way of stewarding your heart and mind, you'll want to share that journey with people who are on the same journey and of the same mindset, people who will encourage you to grow even in difficulties.

Let me just say I'm proud of you for coming this far! Just the fact that you're reading this book tells me a lot about you. It says you have a desire to be all God has for you to be and the willingness to cooperate with Him to reshape your paradigm. You rock!

Be Transformed

*"Do not conformed to the pattern of
this world, but be transformed by the
renewing of your mind. Then you will be
able to test and approve what God's will is —
His good, pleasing and perfect will.."*

Romans 12:2 NIV

For years and years in my Christian journey, I wandered around
thinking thoughts like: "Why doesn't God just make this go
away," or, "If they got healed, then why not me?" or, "What
did I do to deserve this?" Yes, I had my share of rough
beginnings like many people have. I wrote a lot about that in
Unlocking the Heart of the Artist, talking about the struggles I
had with growing up in a religious household yet struggling
with a difficult relationship with my dad, which thankfully has
been restored. Those circumstances and others set me up for

some major roadblocks in my life along with unhealthy coping mechanisms that became my normal operating procedure, or as I termed it in the last chapter, my inner paradigm.

The more I struggled, the more I was frustrated with God because of His seeming unwillingness to take care of these issues for me. I felt unloved and abandoned just trying to survive on a treadmill of performance. To make a long story short, lasting change never came into my life until I realized how God worked in bringing change to my life through renewing my mind.

In my estimation, renewing your mind according to God's Word is the single most important thing you can do to thrive as a son or daughter in the Kingdom, because every other issue that you'll face, without exception, has roots in this issue. If you don't know who you are in Christ, who God really is, what He's said about Himself, your life, your identity, your future, or the enemy, then my friend, you will be tossed around like a feather in the ocean. Hear me now, without learning to renew your mind as empowered and led by the Holy Spirit; you are in for an extremely frustrating and fruitless spiritual journey. That being said, let me show you how this process works!

How Renewing Your Mind Works

Let's take a deeper look at the portion of scripture I shared at the beginning of this chapter. The word "conformed" means "to identify with," so the connotation is, "Don't identify with the way the world does things... the way they think, act, or react." In other words, there's a higher way for us to live rather than to do life just like everyone else does. Remember, if you do what everyone else does then you'll get what everyone else has. I don't know about you, but I want God's best for my life according to His divine design!

So, what's the alternative to conforming? Simple, it's transformation. Now the word "transformed" there in the scripture means, "to change after being with, in keeping with inner reality." Renewing indicates participation in the process of being made new by God's power. The word "mind" in this passage describes your reasoning and thinking faculties. Wow, are you starting to get this?

Think of this in terms of your own life. Scripture is encouraging you not to identify with the way the world does things, but be fundamentally changed through a process of continually encountering God, who ultimately changes your inner reality and affects the way you think and reason. Did you get that? Real, lasting change only happens when we have a continual encounter with Jesus, and He fundamentally transforms the way we think about, feel toward, and experience the world around us.

Why is this necessary? The end of the verse says, "so that you may test and approve (distinguish) what God's will (desire, his best offer) is - - His good, pleasing and perfect will." You see, cooperating with the Holy Spirit to see your mind transformed enables you to develop wisdom in your life, the ability to be able to distinguish what God's best desire for you is within a certain situation. Even in the process of transforming our minds into the likeness of Christ, God is always setting you up to thrive in His Kingdom in line with your divine design. That's incredible.

How Your Inner Paradigm Works

Once you realize that real change is possible by cooperating with the Holy Spirit in this transformative process, life gets pretty exciting. Before we get too far ahead in the process, I want to bring a few things together.

Remember from the last chapter; I told you that you have an inner paradigm that operates your subconscious mind. Many scientists believe that the subconscious is responsible for up to 95% or more of our daily function. Your subconscious controls and affects everything from your breathing to muscle memory as well as your feelings, habits, and responses. Unless you work with the Holy Spirit to see this subconscious mind transformed, you'll be in a continual state of frustration where you want to see change happen but are paralyzed from actually seeing it happen.

Your paradigm lives in your subconscious and is tied to the emotional part of you. You have your mind, which is your conscious thinking apparatus, but your subconscious handles the deep, emotional feeling, sensing part of you on a deep subterranean level. To transform your subconscious paradigm, it takes a couple of things: repetition and emotion. Through the scientific process of what's known as neuroplasticity, we can literally change our brain by changing our thoughts. You can literally wire in new pathways that promote healthy patterns of living and wire out old ones that are toxic. Let's dive a little deeper.

When you and I think, we don't just think in words. For example, if I said, "I want to make a million dollars this year," or, "I want to become a famous artist and have my work sold all over the world," I don't just think in terms of words or numbers, I think it in pictures. I literally begin to see it inside my mind in this beautiful imagination God's given me which begins to form and develop the idea into full maturity. The process of imagining works in harmony with the biological processes that God has installed inside each of us.

When you begin to imagine, you start thinking, then feeling, and all of a sudden, you start seeing the pictures associated with those thoughts and feelings. Those pictures then evoke emotions, and these emotions, together with those thoughts, are what send signals to your brain to start working on behalf of this new idea or goal. All of a sudden, over time with repetition, these new pathways strengthen, and we start to react like second nature within these new pathways. That's how change happens.

See, your brain doesn't care. Your brain will think about anything. Any thought that comes into your mind and is meditated upon, your brain will think about. Your brain is an electrical switching station, and its job is simply to send electrical impulses out to your body and even to others in the sixth sense sort of way you can feel people's energy. That's the job of your brain.

Reticular Activating System

Your brain also has an incredible ability to focus on what it deems important based on your beliefs through what's commonly known as your Reticular Activating System. It's essentially a very complex filtering system that allows your brain to sort through what's important and what's not so that you're not totally overwhelmed by continual stimulus. It does this based on your current belief system, allowing that which supports your beliefs through and filtering out that which doesn't agree.

Most people have heard of this brain system in reference to purchasing a new car. You know the story. You go shopping for and end up purchasing your new dream car only to realize as soon as you drive off the lot that those same cars are everywhere! Funnily enough, you've never really seen them that much before. Why? Your RAS filtered them out until they became important to you. Before you purchased that new car, they were just another unimportant car on the road but now, all of a sudden, they are on your internal radar.

Julie Ann Cairns in her incredible book, *The Abundance Code*, said the following in regards to the RAS and its effect on our life experience:

> *"If we deeply believe something at a subconscious level, then even if we consciously wish things could be different,*

the power of our subconscious mind ensures that our beliefs get reaffirmed again and again in our everyday experiences. In this way, our subconscious beliefs can actually sabotage our conscious efforts to manifest change."

So again, renewing your mind through shifting your internal paradigm to one that is in agreement with what God says about you is vital to experiencing lasting change in your life.

Autopilot & Self-Sabotage

One other feature of note in dealing with your subconscious is that it literally acts as an autopilot system, taking you to a desired destination based on your beliefs. So, for example, if you say you want to have success as an artist financially, creatively, and spiritually, you might, in fact, begin to experience those things, for a while. But then, your internal autopilot system kicks in and says, "Hey, this is not what we really believe. We need to get back on course." And at that point, your subconscious mind will begin to work overtime with your mind, will, and emotions to bring you back to where you're "supposed" to be based on what you really believe.

We have a name for this in the art world, and it's called self-sabotage. Believe me; it's a very real phenomenon. One I've experienced and one I bet you have as well. It feels like a glass ceiling you just can't seem to get beyond. Self-sabotage can even manifest as anxiety, worry, sickness, relational difficulties, and a variety of other barriers designed specifically to get you back into what your subconscious believes is your normal.

Say, for example, you sell the most expensive art piece you've ever sold, all of a sudden, you start having all this fear come up inside your mind. You start thinking crazy thoughts like: "How am I going to pay my taxes? Do I need to spend all this money? Oh, what if they don't like it and they ask for a refund in two weeks?" You might ask, "How do you know all these things, Matt?" Believe me, I know.

All these thoughts of worry, fear and anxiousness start IMAXing on the screen of your mind until, either you acquiesce to those fears through agreement or you kick them to the curb and shift your thoughts to ones in agreement with your new normal in the Kingdom. As you choose to shift your paradigm, you are literally creating new pathways inside your brain. As these new pathways myelinate or insulate over time, they become deeply rooted, allowing your new Godly habits to get stronger, and your subconscious beliefs to shift. It's really incredible how God wired us!

It's Time to Choose

Now that you understand a little more about how your brain and these paradigms work, you have a choice. You can choose what you're allowing to happen in your brain and ultimately what you're experiencing in your life. You can choose to continue operating out of the same old, self-defeating paradigm, or you can begin transforming that old paradigm into one that reflects the nature of Christ and His purposes for your life.

This is so exciting to me, and I hope to you as well! Right now, you can literally turn a new page in your life. You can start to dream, envision, imagine, think the thoughts of the Lord and sow the word of God into your heart right now and change will begin. You can start protecting your heart from the negative thoughts and feelings that come from daily life, like thoughts of lack, sickness, fear, unhappiness, jealousy, and rage, by stopping them at the door of your mind and choosing a new thought. Remember, God's Word says in Philippians 4:8, *"Finally, brothers and sisters, whatever is true, whatever is noble, whatever is right, whatever is pure, whatever is lovely, whatever is admirable—if anything is excellent or praiseworthy—think about such things."* (NIV)

You have a choice, and the Holy Spirit is here right now to empower you so that choice you make will establish a new, healthy pattern in your life!

When you plant the Word of God in your heart, what comes forth? The Kingdom. The Kingdom gets birthed out of that, and the energy of your life begins to resonate with the energy of God. Think about it. We are all made up of light moving at different speeds on different frequencies, that's just the nature of how we were created. I love that, because God's Word says in John chapter 1, that He is life and light as well.

We are literally made of His substance and in His image! Knowing that, we can choose to operate, resonate, and be in harmony with his frequency, or His thoughts and desires for our life, and let that become the paradigm that governs us, or we can operate on a lower level based on woundedness, trauma, old habits, family history, and negative thought patterns. It's your choice.

Birds of a Feather

Let's take it one step further. You've heard that old saying, "Birds of a feather flock together," well that's not just an old wives' tale, that's literally how energy works.

When there are lower frequencies surrounding you, guess what? They literally and scientifically start attracting people those same lower frequencies. The same thing is also true when you are on a higher, more positive frequency that is aligned with the Kingdom of God in your life. What starts to happen? Those people begin to attract higher frequency energy into their life. That's just a scientific fact.

Think of a simple tuning fork and how it works. If a tuning fork is struck, causing it to vibrate and is placed next to another tuning fork in the same key which has not been struck, the second one will begin to vibrate and resonate at the same frequency automatically. How does this happen without the two tuning forks touching one another? Traveling energy known as sound waves. It's a harmonic phenomenon called sympathetic resonance. In fact, I've seen my friend Ray Hughes do the same sort of demonstration by singing into a guitar. As he did, the guitar literally began to resonate with his voice. Such a beautiful picture of how we are designed to resonate with the voice of God.

So literally, when you feel bad, and you start complaining, guess what? You're sending out a resonant frequency, and you can always find somebody to resonate with you! The same is also true if you're cultivating the nature of the Kingdom in your life, staying positive and founded on God's Word, focusing on the vision for your life, and celebrating the good things in your life. When you choose to do this, you are sending out the resonant frequency of Heaven, and you'll begin to see other people like that come into your life as well. It's the power of agreement at work, and it's amazing. All of a sudden you begin to resonate on a frequency that's in harmony with the Kingdom of God, as opposed to that old nature, and you experience life through a completely different set of lenses.

It's been said that you become like the five people you spend the most time with. You should carefully choose who you allow to speak into your life and have an influence on you. God's Word is so clear when it comes to being careful who you choose to allow into the inner circle of your life. This doesn't mean we insulate ourselves from people and the world around us in some sort of elitist manner, but rather act as a wise gatekeeper. Here are just a few verses which encourage you to be wise regarding who you interact with:

- Proverbs 13:20 "Walk with the wise and become wise, for a companion of fools suffers harm." (NIV)

- 1st Corinthians 15:33 "Do not be deceived: "Bad company ruins good character." (NIV)

Through your thoughts and what you believe in your heart, you either resonate with the Kingdom or with that old sinful nature. Now listen, if you get saved, and the Holy Spirit comes to live inside you, and yet you never actively cooperate with Him to change the nature of what's going on inside your heart and mind, then you will be really frustrated. You'll ask questions like, "Is God mad at me?" or, "Why don't things ever work out?" or, "I don't understand why change won't happen in my life." It's because of your paradigm. When you start actively renewing your mind and inviting the Holy Spirit into that process, you will see a physical, tangible change take place in your life. Not just an emotional change, not just a spiritual change. You will literally see physical changes in your life, and that's so exciting!

One of the really exciting things for me is to hear stories of real changes people are experiencing in their life through my Mentoring Program, and this topic, more than any other, is where I see the biggest change happening in people's lives. Once they start actively renewing their mind, it's almost like the curtain opens on the stage of their lives, and they start really living. Creativity starts flowing; sales begin to happen, divine appointments come their way, and life seems to happen on a whole different level. That's my prayer for you as well!

Changing the Vibration of Your Life

I want to give you a few things to help you change the vibration of your life, the way you feel, and what you're focusing on so that you can shift your paradigm and begin to resonate with the Kingdom of God in your life.

One of my favorite quotes in thinking about paradigms is this quote from Andrew Carnegie. He was one of the richest men alive back at the turn of the 20th century, and he said this about how things happen in our mind and get manifested in our life:

"Any idea that is held in the mind that is either feared or revered will at once begin to clothe itself in the most convenient and appropriate physical form available."

I love that. It goes back to what I was describing in Proverbs and now what you know about how the brain works. As you think, as you focus in your mind, so are you in your life. This is so key because the things you focus on get magnified in your life. This is why worship is so important for the believer. We exalt Jesus above everything else, we give Him the highest place and declare His power over everything in our life. Listen, the things that you focus on are the things that you start to imagine and become emotionally connected to. Likewise, the things you get emotionally connected with become thoughts and feelings, literally changing how you feel, the frequency at which you vibrate and resonate.

Think about it. When you meet someone for the first time, you can almost immediately tell if there's a connection or not. How do you know that? Not necessarily by what they say. You just feel it. There's an intuitive discerning sense. What are you feeling? You're literally picking up on the energy that is coming from them. Maybe it's from common interests or background. Maybe they are a Christian, and it's the vibration of the Kingdom that's living inside of them and being transmitted from them.

You've also probably met someone before, and you thought, "I don't know, I just get a weird feeling about this," or, "I just don't connect with this person," or, "There's not any commonality here." Well, what is that? Again, it's the same thing. You're probably on two different frequencies, and all those photons and neutrons are just going bing, bing, bing, "Not a match!" You might understand this intuitively, but I want you to understand that you can change this about yourself in order to feel better, look better, and be in harmony with God's Kingdom. As you start to make these changes, you literally will begin to welcome people and opportunities into your life that are in harmony with the nature of God's plan for your life.

Looking back at my own journey to align with God's best for my life, I can directly connect changes in my life to changes in my paradigm. The big change for me was in 2009 when I began to understand, "Matt, you're an artist, you're a father of artists. God's called you to raise up an army of artists to reveal

His glory to the earth." When I began to align with God's vision for me, what He wanted me to do, who He called me to be, and who He said that I was, everything in my being began to resonate differently. I began intensely focusing on my new vision, and everything else began to take a back seat.

As I changed my focus, guess what started happening? Other people that were resonating with that same thing started being drawn into my life. Other opportunities that I needed all of a sudden were starting to show up in my life. I started feeling better. Things that I had struggled with weren't quite as difficult for me any longer. I could just go on and on and on. Even supernatural finances began to flow into my life. What was that all about? Did God just all of a sudden get in a good mood or did I just start obeying the rules better or what? No. What happened is that the paradigm inside me started to change and I literally began to resonate on a different frequency, one that says, "Father, I get it. Finally, I get who You are and who I am in You and what You have for me, and Lord, I receive now every good thing that you have for me. I'm open to receiving. I let go of all that other stuff." On a daily basis, hour by hour, moment by moment, that's what I started doing, and guess what? Things changed. My normal changed and yours can change too!

Restored to Restore

Through the work of Jesus on the cross, you've been restored. Restored to what?

You've been restored to the reality of being a son or daughter of the Most High God through whom He lives and moves and releases transformation in the earth. You've been restored to a place where sickness and disease are no longer a part of your inheritance. You've been restored to a place where supernatural joy and peace are your portion. You've been restored to a place where you can freely hear the voice of the Lord in the context of relationship, respond to Him, and see Him move through your life in line with your unique design. You've been restored to a place where the financial provision and resources you need to do what He created you to do are assured, not because of what you do or how you perform, but because of who you are! It is this reality that must permeate every fiber of your being, down into your subconscious mind, so that through the Holy Spirit real, lasting change can be established in your life.

Be Transformed

As you discovered at the beginning of this chapter, the word transformation implies that you've been with or had some sort of experience that caused an inner reality shift inside your heart. You see, real transformation always begins with an encounter with God. He changes us, and we respond to Him by affirming what He has done in us. We mirror back to Him through our words and thoughts who He says we are, what we can have, what we can do, and how He's designed us. This repetitive act of recounting the deeds of the Lord and reminding yourself of this new reality is not just trite words spoken. They are literally creating a new reality inside of you. Over time, your heart and subconscious mind begin to trust more in this new reality instead of in the old experience-based reality they've always known.

What Networks Are You Forming In Your Brain?

Acclaimed neuropsychologist Donald Hebb said, "Neurons which fire together, wire together," which essentially means your brain hardwires pathways inside itself to handle tasks on a more efficient basis. By creating these pathways, your brain can quickly determine how to act or react when a certain situation arises. You might experience a situation, and your brain says, "Hey, I've experienced this before, and I know just what to do." And it responds the way it always does.

How does this happen, you might ask? Whenever you have a thought or a feeling, neurons are triggered, and they join together to form a network. As you repeat this process over time, the brain learns to trigger the same neurons and ultimately finds it easy to recall those same thoughts and feelings in similar situations. You have the capacity to literally rewire your brain through repetitive thoughts associated with strong emotions, that will reflect the transformation you want to experience in your life, your new normal.

Think for a moment about addictive behavior. Most of the time, it's simply a learned behavior rooted in some sort of desire to numb the pain that was experienced or perceived to be coming. I'll give you an example. A person is wounded emotionally through a difficult relationship and doesn't have a healthy support system to lean on. He deeply desires help and comfort but doesn't know where to turn. Enter XXX addictive coping mechanism. This "XXX" can be anything you want; food, sex, porn, drugs, emotionalism, victimization, self-harm, etc. Through that situation, the person ends up using XXX, and over time he reinforces that behavior so that his brain learns, "When I feel pain, I do XXX." Make sense? It's not that he is a horrible person or doomed for failure, it's just he's learned a really unhealthy pattern for coping with pain. Change that reaction pattern, and you fundamentally change the person's life. That's why transforming the mind is so important. Remember, as you think, so are you.

Transforming your inner GPS system, your brain's default response system happens through repetition. Your old memories, feelings, and desires are literally replaced over time with new, healthy thoughts. Each thought you create connects with others just like it; remember, thoughts are literally physical things. These thoughts add up to form collections, which in turn form patterns and pathways that create the default operating system within your brain. As you change your thoughts to align with God's thoughts, you are literally transforming your brain to think like God thinks, to have the mind of Christ. As time moves on, your thoughts and responses to things that happen in life will be based in your new identity, not the old.

Well-known Christian cognitive neuroscientist, Dr. Caroline Leaf says in her blog, *Toxic Thoughts*:

"Change in your thinking is essential to detox the brain. Consciously controlling your thought life means not letting thoughts rampage through your mind. It means learning to engage interactively with every single thought that you have, and to analyze it before you decide either to accept or reject it."

For more on the science of this brain-changing process, check out Dr. Caroline Leaf's book, *Switch On Your Brain*.

Faith Comes by Hearing

Bill Johnson said in his book, *Strengthening Yourself in the Lord,* "The key to either great purpose or great destruction lies in where we choose to sustain our focus." Because focus is a function of the brain and thought life, it's important that we train the brain to focus on God's Word and His Kingdom purposes.

In Romans 10:17, the Bible says, "Faith comes by hearing, and hearing by the Word of God." (NKJV) God's Word literally becomes the filter through which everything has to pass through in order to take root in our heart. Until now, if you're like most people you've allowed almost anything into your heart, including thoughts, feelings, experiences, fear, stress, anxiety, and of course, the opinions of others. Now that you understand your role as the gatekeeper of your heart, you can use God's word as a supernatural filter. The wonderful thing about God's Word is that it's powerful. It's not just words on a page; it's sharper than a sword, it never returns void, and will always accomplish that which it was sent for. That's encouraging!

What Seeds Are You Sowing

Not to mix metaphors, but there are two dynamics going on here when we talk about transforming the mind. One is the aspect of being a gatekeeper, only allowing thoughts filtered by God's Word to come into your mind, and the other is that of a gardener who is actively planting seeds and cultivating the ground of your heart. It's not enough to just be on defense, guarding against ungodly thoughts. You have to be actively involved in cultivating the ground of your heart and the planting of new seeds. Otherwise, there won't be any good fruit being produced.

Your seeds determine your fruit. I always tell people you can't be upset about the things you allow in your life. If you're allowing any old thing in, then my friend, any old thing is going to implant itself and start growing. You can't look up one day and say, "Well would you look there! I have no clue how that happened." Sure you do. You allowed it to take root.

You can start today by being led by the Holy Spirit in 'taking every thought captive.' As you do, actively replace negative, ungodly thoughts with thoughts based on God's Word, the dreams He's given you, and His promises over your life. At the same time, ask the Holy Spirit to show you if there are any lies that you've come into agreement within your heart about your creativity, finances, success, or any other area of your life that comes to mind. As He reveals those areas to you, just confess them to Him and ask Him to give you new thoughts with which to replace the lies. It's just like gardening. You've got to get out in the garden, pull those weeds, cultivate the ground, and plant new seeds in order to get flowers to grow. The wonderful thing about gardening is the more flowers your garden produces, the fewer weeds you have! It just takes time and focus. The same is true in your life. As the fruit of God's Word begins to blossom in your life, it creates a new normal by which everything else operates.

Look for the Fruit

One thing people often forget to do as they are planting new thought seeds is to look for the fruit in their life. I've found, depending on the level of faith I have in a certain area, fruit manifests at different times. You never know when something you've believed in will start to sprout in your life, but if you have a clear, Spirit-led vision of where you're going, it shouldn't be that hard to identify what I call "signs of life."

For example, maybe God has given you a vision for selling your art as a full-time artist. You have a clear picture in your mind of what success looks and feels like, and you've even created a vision board around those dreams. You're also taking time every day to reinforce that vision through Spirit-led visualization and scripture-based affirmations. As this becomes your new normal, be on the lookout for people, places, opportunities, and resources that are a fit. Knock on doors, step out in faith, and pursue opportunities as the Spirit guides you towards divine appointments. It's in those places of supernatural connection, those people you "shouldn't" have met, the discount that just "happened" to be on the day you walked in, or the opportunity that was offered to you before anyone else, that's what fruit looks like. I can't wait to hear your story of how God starts birthing fruit in your life through this process!

To aid you in your quest of being transformed, I've reserved the free resource, Daily Affirmations to Build Your Faith, just for you. You can access this powerful tool and a few others at:

www.MattTommeyMentoring.com/cttfree

Be Fruitful & Multiply

*"God blessed them and said to them,
"Be fruitful and increase in number, fill
the earth and subdue it. Rule over the fish in
the sea and the birds in the sky and over every
living creature that moves on the ground."*

Genesis 1:28 NIV

One of the biggest frustrations I hear from artists no matter where I am in the world is the fact they feel things aren't progressing fast enough in their own creative journey. They see the vision of where they want to be creatively, spiritually, and financially, but for reasons unknown to them at the time, they just can't seem to see good fruit. The result is a feeling of frustration and anxiety that leaves them paralyzed to make any change in their life.

Realize that dissatisfaction can actually be a creative state. I know that might seem counterintuitive, but it's true! When you're feeling dissatisfied, your heart is actually telling you, "Hey, this is not okay, something needs to change." The problem isn't with being dissatisfied but with how you choose to respond to the feelings of dissatisfaction in your life. Most people allow those feelings to emotionally overwhelm them, leading to increased feelings of anxiety about their situation. This leads to circular patterns of frustration, only serving to dig you deeper into a hole of unhappiness. And as you probably already know, that's not helping anyone!

The healthier way to respond to dissatisfaction is to lean in, look it squarely in the eye, and ask the Holy Spirit to help you understand what about this particular situation needs to change. Remember, His role in all this is as our guide. He is the one who leads us into all Truth. Once you start to embrace dissatisfaction as an invitation to change, you can actually begin to create a pathway forward based on faith and vision rather than in fear. That, my friend, is how you begin to see Kingdom fruitfulness manifest in your life.

You might be asking, "Matt, what does being dissatisfied have to do with fruitfulness manifesting in my life, I don't get it?" Well, I'm glad you asked because fruit development is an interesting process. Let's look at this in terms of your own creative process.

How Does Fruit Develop?

The first thing you need for fruit to be produced happens way before there's even a thought of fruit; it's called a seed. A seed contains absolutely everything it needs to become a fully mature plant that can produce fruit. It's how the seed was created. The only thing a seed requires to begin the sprouting process is the right environment. Otherwise, a seed can just sit there for years and years, full of potential, but never blossom into the plant which it was created to be.

Okay, so, you've got a seed, and that seed needs to go into the right environment in order for it to go through the natural process required to bring forth growth, and ultimately, its fruit. This sounds like such a lovely process, right? Not really. In fact, for the seed to begin to sprout, grow, bud, and fruit, it first has to go into a time of darkness. All alone the seed sits there in the dark earth and sheds its protective coating in the dirt. Eventually, it transforms into something so much more than its original state. The seed doesn't physically die per se because the seed embryo is still full of life. Rather, the seed sheds its old form in order to transform into a new state of being, that of a fruit producing plant. Given the right environment of warmth, water, nutrients, and light, the fledgling seed will begin to sprout, grow, and mature, eventually producing fruit. Unless the seed goes through this process, there's absolutely no way fruit is ever going to be produced. It's just how God designed the process.

The same type of process holds true in your life as well. You have seeds of greatness, seeds of divine design implanted within you by God. As you die to your own understanding of how these seeds should produce and mature, over time, you will see them produce fruit as you nurture them through an intimate relationship with the Lord.

I watch this process take place in the lives of artists who I'm privileged to walk within my Created to Thrive artist mentoring program. They come into the program full of hope and vision for the promise of a breakthrough on their creative journey and start to realize that there's a shedding that has to take place. Old mindsets, feelings, and habits have to be shed in order for the seeds inside them to burst forth with life. No matter how much they want to see that seed sprout, it's not going to do anything unless that old shell is shed. One of the artists recently shared this with me:

> *"Growing up as an introvert my mother overprotected me from my fears and anxiety of the outside world, and having an alcoholic dad did not help. I chose to retreat into my own world where it was safe, that safe place was being creative. Art was how I communicated without words when I struggled talking or socializing. As an adult my paradigm caused me to fear to stepping out and following my dreams.*

> *Fear had a grip on me. I even had trouble looking people in the eyes and struggled with self-worth which kept me from success. Then came a rough marriage where I*

thought I found someone who would love and protect me from life's challenges, not so it became a nightmare of abuse that lasted 24 years before it ended in divorce. All of this affected my concept of who I was, and it dried up my love for art.

Over the years God slowly helped me become stronger. It's been a slow journey. Now years later I've learned to trust the Lord, in the process, and in the journey. March 2017 became a huge turning point in my life when I found the Created to Thrive Mentoring Group. I finally had a place to feel safe, be accepted, and to grow in my creativity and the truth of who I am.

Wow, it was like God propelled me forward with great speed as my dry bones come to life. I have grown more in that last 7 months than I have in the past 7 years! The fear is getting smaller and smaller, and I'm creating like never before. I'm even feeling more comfortable with who I am, and with being around people, I'm socializing more with ease. Family and friends keep telling me they see a big difference in my confidence and boldness. My art style even shows a difference.

Now that I am retired, I ask myself, "can I even follow my dreams now?" YES, I CAN! My best years are yet to come. I'm so grateful for this group, for Matt's teachings and the solid Christian faith and truths he gives us, for the endless tools and info to move me forward in art and in business, for the encouragement and community with other group members, and for finding amazing friends *who get me! This past November I had a booth at a local art show, I sold a painting for $200.00! I love this new mindset of Confidence!"* C. Johnson

Having to shed the old has been the case in my own life as well. Every time I'm about to move into a season where new seeds start sprouting, it's always preceded by a time of creative dissatisfaction, darkness, and releasing of old paradigms. It's just the way God works in our life, and it's a beautiful process. It draws us closer to Him, helps us to hear his voice more clearly, and it prepares us for a new season of fruitfulness. Otherwise, we'd try our best to go into the new season holding on to everything from the past, and that simply doesn't work.

Creative Fruit

Now, this process also happens in our creative life as well. When God gives us creative inspiration and ideas for new creative expression to pursue in our artistic journey, He does so in the form of seeds. These seeds come to us in the form of nudgings, prophetic unction, pictures, or feelings that we might or might not understand at the time. Don't you wish you just got a nice, tidy download in a PDF format from the Father saying, "Matt, this is exactly what you should do, now go..." Unfortunately, it rarely happens that way with such clarity. Rather, as the Holy Spirit moves on us with inspiration, He empowers us with grace to start the process of discovery.

Mark Virkler, in his groundbreaking book, *How to Hear God's*

Voice, expressed this concept with such clarity when he said: "Forty-nine percent of the New Testament contains references to spiritual (non-rational) experiences. To be bound by rationalism will effectively cut off half of New Testament Christianity. If you are not relating intuitively to God, but only intellectually, you will lose your opportunity to flow in the nine gifts of the Holy Spirit; to receive guidance through dreams and visions; to have a fully meaningful and effective prayer life; to commune with the Lord in a dialogue, to build an extremely intimate relationship with Him; and to wholly experience the inward benefits of true worship... We must rediscover direct contact with God and once again become open to intuitive, spiritual experiences."

Ultimately, that Spirit-born inspiration is interpreted through our unique creative voice under the leading of the Holy Spirit, and it expresses itself through our skills, experience, and preferences. Many artists who are Christian don't yet understand that believing somehow every creative unction from the Holy Spirit will be interpreted and expressed in the same way, or through their natural understanding, when in fact, the opposite is true. I love the fact that because the Holy Spirit could be saying the same exact thing to five different people at the same time, there could be five different interpretations of that inspiration based on the creative voice of the person releasing that expression. How beautiful! Co-laboring with the Holy Spirit in our creative process is not about robotically replicating exact directions, but rather being inspired by the movement of the Spirit within us and expressing that inspiration with the freedom of a son or daughter.

The challenge for many artists is that in their excitement to share what God just showed them, they neglect to plant the seed. Instead of allowing the seed to go through the natural process of going into the ground, shedding its outer protective coating, sprouting, budding, growing, and fruiting, they just give it their best shot and create something quickly that resembles the seed they just received.

Some might think that this is exactly how the process is supposed to work. First, you get the inspiration, and then you get it out as quickly as possible. I suggest that this way of operating actually cuts off the fruitfulness God designed for that seed. It's like giving away seeds but calling it fruit. See, when you give away seeds, they give no nourishment to those receiving them, only the promise of nourishment once the seed's full potential is released. However, when you give away fruit, you give away nourishment, refreshment, and the promise of more through the seeds contained within the fruit itself. Do you see why our job in the Kingdom is to produce fruit?

This might challenge your concept of how the creative process works, but that's okay. See, divine inspiration is meant to be planted inside your heart, your creative well, so your heart can incubate the idea in concert with the movement of the Holy Spirit. As you do this over time, more clarity will come, and more ideas will start to burst forth as the plant starts to grow. If you stay in this process, the initial idea you had will develop into a mature, fruit producing plant that can now be shared with others, allowing them to partake in the goodness of God through your creative process. Is this making sense?

The desire to immediately share the seeds of inspiration, instead of

allowing them to marinate and mature into fruit, not only cuts off the potential impact of your artistic work (or any Spirit-born idea), but it also robs you of growing through the creative process. Instead of wrestling in your art making and learning to cooperate with the movement of the Spirit through uncharted territory, this is simply choosing the quick, immature expression in order to move on to the next thing.

Fruit from Abiding in the Vine

Let's consider another facet of how fruit happens in our life. Jesus talked about it as well, and it's by abiding in the vine.

Here's how Jesus described this process in John 15:

"I am the true vine, and my Father is the vinedresser. ² Every branch in me that does not bear fruit he takes away, and every branch that does bear fruit he prunes, that it may bear more fruit. ³ Already you are clean because of the word that I have spoken to you. ⁴ Abide in me, and I in you. As the branch cannot bear

fruit by itself, unless it abides in the vine, neither can you, unless you abide in me.⁵ I am the vine; you are the branches. Whoever abides in me and I in him, he bears much fruit, for apart from me you can do nothing. ⁶ If anyone does not abide in me he is thrown away like a branch and withers; and the branches are gathered, thrown into the fire, and burned. ⁷ If you abide in me, and my words abide in you, ask whatever you wish, and it will be done for you. ⁸ By this my Father is glorified, that you bear much fruit and so prove to be my disciples. ⁹ As the Father has loved me, so have I loved you. Abide in my love. ¹⁰ If you keep my commandments, you will abide in my love, just as I have kept my Father's commandments and abide in his love. ¹¹ These things I have spoken to you, that my joy may be in you, and that your joy may be full. ¹² This is my commandment, that you love one another as I have loved you." (ESV)

I love this passage of scripture! In fact, it was the first message I ever preached back when I was a teenager in Georgia, but I digress. Everything in the Kingdom is birthed out of a relationship with the Father, through Jesus, by the Holy Spirit working in our life. It's all about intimacy with Him. The word "abide," or in some translations "remain," means literally to wait, continue, endure, last, or stay. It literally implies time and the willingness to remain in the middle of hardship, misunderstanding, frustration, and uncomfortableness.

If you're like me, I know you can relate to situations like this in your life, times where you had to stay, but out of that staying came huge fruit. You know this, but it's important to emphasize the fact that real, lasting fruit happens in our life when we stay the course in our relationship with Jesus. Otherwise, we bounce to and fro from situation to situation, wondering why nothing happens in our life, becoming frustrated, and ultimately giving up.

More on How Fruit is Produced

Let me break this passage down for you. First of all, Jesus explains if we're producing fruit, we can expect to be pruned in order to produce more fruit. That's just part of the natural course of being a branch. Secondly, He reminds us that any lasting fruit that's being born into our life can only happen through our relationship with Him and that through that relationship, we will bear what he calls "much fruit." See, there Jesus goes again being all abundance minded! More than you can ask or imagine. Big impact. Much fruit! That's our portion in the Kingdom.

If you're like me, you can think back to times in your life when you got ahead of the Lord and tried to produce fruit on your own. I remember when God first called me as a father to artists, to raise up an army of artists, back in 2009. He poured out such revelation and favor during that season that when the season changed, I tried to keep going on yesterday's revelation and way of doing things rather than keeping in step with the new thing He was doing.

God had supernaturally given me a building for our ministry in

2009 when we lived in metro Atlanta, so when He moved us to Asheville, North Carolina, I was convinced He was going to do the same thing here. So, I figured I'd help him out! I started looking for every vacant building I could find. I was prophesying over the buildings and gathering other artists for a big vision all based on how God had done it in the previous season, when, in fact, the Father had something completely different in mind. Thank goodness the Holy Spirit redirected me and nudged me back on course because I know all too well what we start in our own strength, we have to maintain in our own strength. However, when God births the fruit, we get the benefit of His grace to walk through the process with Him, yielding much more fruit than we ever could by ourselves.

Asking Out of Intimacy

Now, the next part of this scripture is simply amazing to me, because it shows what normal relationship with the Father is supposed to be about! He actually tells us that when we are abiding in Him through genuine relationship, we can ask whatever we want, and it will be done! WOW! Did you get that? Come on, somebody, this is powerful! Not only will the Father be the one producing fruit through our lives, but we also get to participate in the process, dreaming, asking, receiving, and co-laboring with Him to see His Kingdom come, and His will be done in the earth as it is in Heaven. Wow, just, wow!

It even gets better, because He goes on to say: "By this my

Father is glorified that you bear much fruit and so prove that you are my disciples." By what? By abiding in Him and asking whatever we want. WOW again! Jesus is literally saying that this kind of crazy faith, birthed in intimacy with the Father, is what brings glory to the Father and proves that we are His disciples. If that's true, then the opposite is also true: if you and I don't abide and don't ask because of fear, based in our past or old paradigms, then we can't be His disciples.

Abiding, imagining, asking, agreeing, and receiving is the way of the Kingdom. Whether it's in your daily life or your artistic expression, there's no other way. Lasting fruit happens when we abide in Him, allow our imagination to be ignited and led by the Holy Spirit, ask the impossible, receive what He shows us and then respond with the gifts and talents He's invested in us within our circle of influence.

Producing Fruit in Your Art

Now that you understand how this fruitfulness process works in your art let's transfer that understanding into your life because it works in exactly the same way. Whether it's your finances, relationships, health, or any number of issues facing you, the way you experience fruitfulness is the same. Start with intimacy and ask the Holy Spirit to stir your imagination to dream with Him. Constantly invite Him into your daily life and creative musings. Ask Him to fill you with inspiration as you actively seek to fill your own creative well by doing things that bring you life and give you a sense of awestruck wonder. As you're inspired, say yes to the inspiration and begin to create as the Spirit leads you, developing your skills along the way. Let me clarify. This doesn't mean that you sit around waiting for the heavens to part and angels to appear until you start creating and living life. Rather, it means that as you live and create on a daily basis, you listen for His leading and follow it; co-creating with Him. As you do, His voice becomes more natural, and listening becomes much more intuitive.

Multiplication & Authority

Let's take this one step further. Remember, the scripture in Genesis said that God blessed them to be fruitful, to multiply, and then to steward the earth they had been given authority over. This is key for you to understand because most of the time, people are confused why they don't have multiplication or authority in their life in certain areas, and it causes frustration. Well, let me tell you exactly why. It's because they are short-circuiting the process.

Everything in your life begins with the blessing of God. Realize what the Bible teaches us in 2nd Peter 2, that God has blessed you with everything you need for life and godliness. In Him, you have need of nothing. Nothing! The fruitfulness you want to experience in your life comes out of the blessing you've received in the context of your relationship with Jesus. Once you begin bearing fruit, then multiplication is the natural result. You can't have multiplication and increase in your life that has any eternal impact without Spirit-birthed fruitfulness. Blessing leads to fruitfulness, fruitfulness leads to multiplication, and then multiplication leads to authority. The best you can hope to do on your own is to create carnal fruit that will only last for a while and then rot. Let's not go there.

If you've ever heard me speak before, you'll know I love telling people that in order to be a great artist, you have to make a lot of ugly art. It's true! You rarely get to the great unless you go through the awkward and ugly. The key is not staying there, but moving through that process into creative maturity. Think of it as a cross-country airplane trip. You want the awkward and ugly stage to be a short layover, not your final destination. Your destination is fruitful beauty!

Do you want authority in your life and art? Do you want to see multiplication in your finances or the impact of your creative expression? Then, my friend, you first have to be fruitful with what's in your hand now. Over time, as you stick with the process, you'll start to see authentic fruit develop that will be so much more than you ever dreamed possible, and it will be enough to replenish you, refresh others, and give you an overwhelming amount of seed for the next season.

Faithful with Little, Ruler over Much

Well done, good and faithful servant. You have been faithful over a little; I will set you over much. Enter into the joy of your master. **Matthew 25:23 ESV**

As I've mentioned previously, one of my favorite portions of scripture is Matthew 25 and the Parable of the Steward. More than any other parable Jesus taught, it clearly illustrates how the Father both invests in each of us and expects us to grow that investment over time. Not only that, it's a primer on how to grow in influence and impact in the Kingdom of God.

This wonderful story begins with the master coming to the field and gathering his three servants together. Basically, he says, "Hey guys, I am going on a journey, and it's going to be a pretty long one, and while I'm gone, I am entrusting you with a certain amount of money," which he called talents. With these talents, the master was essentially investing in each one of them for the time he was planning to be away. He's encouraging and equipping them to go do what he called them to do, invest the talents he gave them along the way and be prepared to return the money with growth when he returns. The story then says to one guy he gave five talents, to one he gave two talents, and to the last he gave one talent.

In Matthew 25:19, the story continues, "Now after a long time the masters of servants came in and settled accounts with them." Evidently, the master was back from his trip and went to check on his guys and their return on his investment. It goes on, "He who received five talents came forward bringing five talents more," saying to him, "Master you delivered to me five talents, here I've made five talents more," and his master said to him, "Well done good and faithful servant. You've been faithful with the little. Now I'm going to make you ruler over much. Enter into the joy of your master." If you're the first guy, I'd say you're having a pretty good day at this point. You doubled your master's money, you got a promotion, and everyone's happy.

As the story continues, the master says the same thing to the guy to whom he gave two talents, since he doubled his money as well, bringing four talents: "Well done good and faithful servant. You have been faithful over little; I am going to make you ruler over much." Again, the second guy is having a very good day.

Now, I'm just going to stop here for a second. Whether you realize it or not, a central tenet of understanding of how you grow in the Kingdom of God has just been revealed within those few little words. What words might you ask? The words: "You have been faithful over little, now I will make you ruler over much." Let that sink in for a second as we dig into this concept.

What's In Your Hand?

Over the years, whether I am speaking to or mentoring artists who are searching for direction, I have always encouraged them to ask the Lord to show them what's currently in their hands. It's very common for we dreamers always to be looking from the thirty-thousand-foot view rather than looking for the things that we have with which we've been currently entrusted. It's more exciting to see the big picture, to dream big, and to pray big prayers like, "God, give me the nations." If that's you, let me just take a moment to encourage you. It's incredibly important that we dream and see the big picture in our life because otherwise, we can get caught in the details and lose sight of where we're going. However, it's also vital to understand; the only way vision manifests into reality is if you are faithful with what you have now.

One of the artists who's in my mentoring group shared a

similar story with me and the importance of realizing what was in her hand. Here's her story:

"Several years ago my Mom died after a 3 year battle with cancer, and I was her caregiver. Several months before she left, I tried acrylic painting, to occupy my time and emotions. I had been an artist for years, but life got in the way. I was focused on family, ministry and an administrative career. My mom's final words to me were that her only regrets were not going after her creative gifts. Ironically, she said she was so proud of me for going after mine.

After her death, the Lord began to speak to me about my deepest dreams and passions (I really thought I was already living my dream by serving Him). Something stirred in me that it might involve art, but I actually told my husband I didn't like to do art because it made me "feel bad." Well, long story short - I'm shocked at what the Lord has opened up for me in this past 6 months. After struggling for a couple of years about "finding my dream," I read a book by a friend that challenged me to live a fearless life. It was then that I realized my greatest fears and insecurities revolved around my art skills. Within a week of that challenge, I stumbled across Matt Tommey's mentoring group. After one day of a trial subscription, I knew it was God's answer to my prayers, and I signed up! In the first couple of lessons, Matt addressed the fears I had about pursuing art and the fears about finances connected to art. It was such a shocker to me - how had that been buried in me for so long and I didn't even know it! How did I not see what is so obvious to me now?

I'm still working a full-time job, but I've produced more artwork in the past four and one-half months that I had in 25 years. I've had new pieces in three art shows and recently sold a handful of prints from one of my paintings. And I feel like I haven't even started yet. I'm still working with Holy Spirit on my vision and my style. But my primary focus is enjoying painting and building a cohesive body of work. What's in my hand right now? Paint! Paint! Paint! I've had a couple of bumps in the road, but the weekly teachings and archived resources are keeping me on track and opening up all kinds of new ideas and possibilities. So the bumps have actually turned into learning tools instead of paralyzing me like they've done most of my life! And my interaction with the group is so very encouraging! I've had heartfelt connections with other artists in the Mastermind Groups, and I found a group member that lives near me. We've met a couple of times for coffee/lunch. We're having a blast getting together and talking about Matt's teachings and the process we are in. It's incredible to share this journey with people who understand and are going on a similar journey!" B. Farmer

Right now, even as you're reading this book, take a few

minutes and ask the Lord to show you what's in your hand now: what skills you have, what opportunities you have, what relationships you have, what amount of money you have, what time you have, and what talents you have. See, all of those things are the "talents" God has invested in your life up to this point. Even though the story talks about talents in the context of money, it's perfectly reasonable to read this passage in the larger context of God's investment in you as His son or daughter.

My friend, if you want to grow in the Kingdom and grow into the fullness of the vision the Holy Spirit is hopefully revealing to you as you read this book, then you have to understand this concept. As you begin to gain understanding and confidence on your journey of stewarding God's investment in your life, you're going to see some incredible things begin to manifest. Why? Because that's how the Kingdom works. Every week as you walk with the Lord in faith, you'll grow in clarity and confidence. As you are faithful with the little amount of what He reveals to you, you'll begin to notice more opportunities, resources, relationships, and ideas coming your way. Why? You're on a continual promotion track. You're being faithful with the little the Father originally entrusted to you, and now He's ready to entrust you with more. That's the normal flow of the Kingdom.

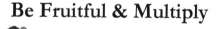 ## Be Fruitful & Multiply

It's just like in the Genesis story of the

Garden of Eden where the Lord says to Adam and Eve, "Be fruitful and multiply and subdue the earth." That's a principle in the God's Kingdom. If you want to multiply and have growth, you first have to be fruitful with what you have. You can't multiply without fruitfulness, and if you try to do it in your own strength, you'll end up creating a big mess, eventually crying out to God to come clean it up! Learn to grow the right way by being fruitful and faithful with the little. Then, you'll get to watch God be faithful to exponentially multiply your efforts into more than you could ever ask or imagine.

It's so common these days, even among well-meaning believers, to be out there trying their best to grow and multiply their efforts in whatever circle of influence God has placed them into while never being fruitful in what God has given them. The reason this is a big deal, and one that can completely thwart the work of the Lord in your life, is because you can't share, teach, or impart anything in this life with any authority outside of the things that God has already worked in your life. Otherwise, you are simply sharing shallow ideas about potentially really great things without the authority to act or the anointing to impart.

One of the reasons I believe *Unlocking the Heart of the Artist* has gone and continues to go all over the world and touch so many people is not because ole Matt is such a good writer. It's because ole Matt went through a bunch of crap in his life, messed up a lot, got on the healing train, and tried to do what the Lord showed him. I'm still learning how to respond to what the Lord shows me every day in my own journey of unlocking.

I've learned that it's out of those difficult places we learn how to respond to the Lord and have Him produce fruit in our life. It's out of those places that the Lord gives authority and revelation to go deeper and do more. Trust God to produce fruitfulness in your life first, and then let Him multiply it. The beautiful thing is, when you give away Spirit-birthed fruit, you give away nourishment for right now, refreshing for right now, and the opportunity to multiply in the future, because fruit contains seeds.

This is such a beautiful picture of how discipleship works. I am going to meet your need. I am going to encourage you now. I am going to feed you now but also within this. I'm going to give you the seeds to do this thing yourself. As you experience the process, you'll get to minister and multiply the process.

Good & Faithful

I just love it where the Master tells the first two guys, "Well done good and faithful servants." The word "good" there means intrinsically good which gets back to the foundational concept of identity in the Kingdom. We are not good or good enough because of what we do; we are good because of who we are. We're worthy and worth celebrating because of who He says we are because of our relationship with the Father through Jesus.

He also calls them "faithful," which means that they were fully persuaded in believing. Again, it's not all about doing works in order to be found worthy, but it's about knowing your heart has been fully renewed and transformed in such a way that the things that God says about you and your calling are so entrenched inside you, that you are faithful to them. You can be faithful to that realization because it's not something that's going to be changed by the wind. It's something that is locked down and imprinted in you because the Holy Spirit is fundamentally transforming you by the renewing of your mind.

This is so important for you to get! A renewed mind and a heart that is fully convinced of its new identity are the essential foundations in growing in the Kingdom. You can't do anything in the Kingdom worth any eternal value without those two things.

Jesus continues, saying, "You've been faithful over little, now I am going to make you ruler over much." The word ruler as used in this phrase actually means to sit in an office or position with authority. As you are faithful to the little things that God has for you, He will start positioning you in places of authority where you can be His ambassador. In that position of influence, you can offer to others what God's done in your life, call those things that are not as though they already are, speak the healing word of life into situations going on in the lives of people, and make a real Kingdom impact.

This is the way the Kingdom works, and it only expands in your life as you continue on the road of being fruitful and multiplying as led by the Spirit. One of the reasons I love this story in Matthew 25 is because the master gave each of these people a different level of investment based on their ability. On their ability, you might be wondering? Yes! in verse 15 it says, "To one he gave five talents, to another two, to another one, to each according to his ability." (ESV)

See, this wasn't some sort of spiritual socialism where everybody gets the same thing. No, in fact, one guy received five talents, one received two, and one fellow received one. Interestingly, it didn't say in the story exactly what the experience criteria was, but we can gather from understanding the whole story that the person who received the five talents had shown himself more faithful or faithful for a longer period of time than the other guys. There it is again, faithful with little, ruler over much.

He Went at Once

One other note about a phrase in verse 16; it says, "He who had received five talents went at once and traded with them and made five talents more." (ESV) When did he go? He went at once, with no delay. It doesn't say that about the other two guys, but to me, it's a glaring detail. People who have grown in maturity in the Lord and in their gifting over the years realize the importance of the now. When God gives you something, do it now. Don't wait, but rather learn to move while there's grace to move. As you do, you will be able to seize opportunities that are there for that moment but might shortly dissipate. I've learned over the years as you grow in the Lord, your confidence level to move quickly increases.

Let me share just a quick story about moving quickly in response to the word of the Lord. Back around 2014, I was in the middle of trying to get my art career off the ground. I had opened a studio with a friend in Asheville's River Arts District but frankly, was doing what everyone else was doing to get business in the luxury craft market. Prevailing opinion at that point was that if you wanted to sell to and be found by high-end fine craft buyers, you had to be at the big, important shows which included shows in places like SOFA in Chicago, the Philadelphia Museum of Art, the Smithsonian, the American Craft Council, and others, so that's what I was doing. I had applied to all the big shows and gotten in some and was rejected by some others. That's normal.

In March of that year, I had invested about $3,500 to participate in the America Craft Council Show in Baltimore. It was expensive because it was a high-end show, far away from my home which required me to have a hotel for five nights plus travel, meals, etc. You get the picture. I remember going up there full of faith to have a $15,000+ show. I was stoked. What happened was less than stellar. At the end of the show, I barely made enough to cover my expenses. Needless to say, I was extremely frustrated.

On the way home, as I was driving, I started expressing my frustration to the Lord. If you close your eyes, you can probably hear me now, whining all the way down the Shenandoah Valley! As I did, the Lord so patiently began to speak to my heart. He began reminding me of several things He had spoken to my heart previously including two major facts. The first was He had given me the studio in the River Arts District, and I needed to get it ready to sell, which I interpreted to mean prepare it to be a beautiful retail space. At that time, my studio in the River Arts District was a bohemian paradise, but we weren't really selling much of anything. Secondly, He reminded me of the fact that He had given me my baskets to give me life, not to be my life. This was a real wake up call for me, because I had gotten the proverbial cart before the horse and was letting art sales and my desire to grow my art business get in front of what God wanted to do in my life. It was one of those spiritual recalibrations we all need from time to time.

Then He reminded me of one more thing. He told me, "Matt, I told you that if you trusted me on this journey that I would bring you the clients so that when you travel, it would be for ministry and pleasure, not to sell your work." That was a big shift for me, but I knew it was the Lord, so I relented in my heart. By the time I got home, I had a plan in my heart to redo the studio and start this next leg of the journey.

I came home, and we started feverishly working on the studio to modify the space into more of a retail gallery in the front and working studio in the back. I invested about $1,500, which at that time was a lot of money, and prayed we were on the right track. We installed new lights, new pedestals, painted some new walls, and even a faux fireplace. It was a lot of work in a short period of time, but I remember I finished on a Thursday, and we had an artist retreat that weekend. Since I wasn't teaching on that Saturday, the thought occurred to me: "I'll just go up to the studio today." I had been there all day without much traffic and then about 3:30pm, as I was thinking about leaving early, a couple walked in. They began to share with me that they were from Atlanta and had planned to come to see my work in Baltimore at the show a couple of weeks ago but weren't able to come, so they drove up from Atlanta today to see my work. There on the spot, they commissioned a $2,000 single basket and paid me a 50% deposit before they left. I was floored! The wonderful thing about this story is that it was just the beginning. That process of trusting the Lord is still how I do business to this day with even greater results!

But Matt, are you saying all I have to do is just trust Jesus, and He'll bring me the clients I need to buy my art? What I'm saying is that when you, just like the man with five talents in the story, respond quickly to the Word of the Lord in your life, whatever that might be, you can always trust God to be faithful to His Word. Of course, you need to be out there every day doing things like building relationships, creating beautiful work, meeting new people, interacting with people on social media, and optimizing your website. Yes, you need to work hard, but it's not up to you to produce the results. That's up to God.

Your responsibility is to steward well the investment He's put inside of you, and then follow His lead. Every person has a different path as each grows his business, but it's vital that you respond to the voice of the Lord and follow His lead in the unique context of your life, art, and business. The more you respond, and respond quickly, to the voice of the Lord, the more faith develops around that process in your own heart. That's how you mature.

In verse 21 and 23, after the Master tells the two servants what a good job they've done and how they've been faithful with little and how they now are being made ruler over much, He says, "Enter into the joy of your master."(ESV) This is huge, because joy and fulfillment in your life, along with abundance financially, resources, relationships, and new ideas, are all found when you steward well the calling and resources God has given you. Again, when you are plugged into who God has designed you to be and what God has uniquely designed you to do, you can enter fully into the joy of your Master. I love that!

Don't Be That Guy

Now the story brings us to the third guy; there is always a third guy, right? And in verse 24 it says, "The one who had received one talent came forward saying…,"(ESV) or in some translations, it says, "He came running." Either way, when I imagine this story, I think about that someone who says they are going to do something that just ends up dropping the ball. Then, the next time you see them, they either totally hide from you or they come up spouting excuses a mile a minute like, "Well, you know my cat died...my car broke down...the dog ate my homework... I had a flat tire." Excuses, excuses, excuses; you get the picture.

Well, that's kind of what we see in the situation here in verse 24. He received one talent, and on the day when the Master returned, he ran up to the Master saying, "Master, I knew you to be a hard man, reaping where you did not sow and gathering where you did not scatter seed, so I was afraid, and I went and hid your talent in the ground. Here, you have what is yours." (ESV)

You might be putting the puzzle pieces together, especially after reading the earlier chapter based on the passage in Proverbs, "As a man thinks in his heart, so is he." You see, what this guy believed about the Master directly impacted his ability to be faithful with what he had been given. This is huge! Think about it. The Master of the field had put him in the field; He had given him His well-funded trust, authority, and everything the servant needed to thrive. So, what was the only thing stopping this guy at this point? It was his belief. It was what he believed about his Master and what he believed about himself in relation to the Master.

Anytime you operate out of a place of fear, it paralyzes you, and it stops you from being able to be fruitful. You go into protection mode and become like a turtle, tucking its head into its shell, or like an ostrich with his head in the sand. When you let fear rule, you are not able to walk into the fullness of your calling in the Kingdom, and friend, Jesus takes this very seriously. It's not like He said, "Oh well, poor baby, you know you can just keep that talent." No, He called him a wicked and slothful servant, and not only was the Master unhappy with the servant, but He took back His money, and He gave it to the guy who had returned back ten talents.

This concept is really important to understand, not in a shame-filled, religious way that says, "I'm so bad. I've totally screwed this up." Just realize when God invests something in you, or when the Holy Spirit brings an idea to you and puts something in your hand, it's serious because it's not just about you. It's about His Kingdom going forth. You're His ambassador in the earth within your circle of influence.

You know, I can tell you with great certainty, like when God told me in 2009 at 3:09 am that He was calling me as a father to artists, to go to the nations and raise up an army of artists to reveal his Glory in the earth. He told me my calling was ministry and marketplace both full time. I can tell you, at the time I was completely confused about how that was going to flesh itself out. I didn't understand how I could work a full-time job and work in ministry at the same time. I didn't have context for what the Father was telling me, but I knew it was significant. Even though I didn't understand all the details of how it would work itself out, I can tell you with great certainty that there has been no greater season of joy and fulfillment, abundance, and fruitfulness in my life than these last years. Why? Because I'm connecting with who God has called me to be. Do I do everything right all the time? Absolutely not. I screw it up. I make wrong decisions. I react out of a place of fear, just like you do, from time to time, but I've learned and have convinced my heart that it's not a zero-sum game. I am moving from glory to glory to glory. I am on this Holy Ghost train moving up, and up, and up. Every time I fall, I get right back up and keep going. Why? Because I have determined in my heart, by the grace of God, I am not going to live my life out of a place of fear, shame, or control any longer. Listen, when you operate out of fear, you end up being "that guy," the third guy in the story, and you literally quench what God wants to release in and through your life. Don't be that guy.

Growing in God's Kingdom

Jesus grew in wisdom and in stature,
and in favor with God and man.
Luke 2:52 NIV

Having grown up in a religious family, I had a view of God that was very much tied to performance, obeying the rules, and being seen as godly. In youth group, we were always rededicating and repenting to make sure we were clean enough to be used by God. This kind of performance-based lifestyle was exhausting and had lots of baggage with it that has taken years to overcome. I'm so thankful now that each of us have come to a much more grace-filled approach to life and faith! However, you might have experienced some of those same patterns as well. When I started learning about growing in God's Kingdom, it was natural for me to think of it in terms of performance or that it was tied to my salvation, but in reality, nothing could be further from the truth. Let me share some foundational truths with you about how growth in the Kingdom really happens.

The Result of Intimacy

Growth in the Kingdom has nothing to do with your salvation because you don't get more or less saved trying to work for your salvation or perform for God. Growth in the Kingdom is the natural outcome of walking in the Spirit as someone who is saved by grace through faith in Jesus. However, as you walk faithfully with the Lord and steward well what He puts into your hands, He will produce fruit in your life. That's His promise. As fruit is produced in your life and you continue to plant the seeds He gives you, things grow, we expand, and God's Kingdom expands. That's how it works. That's called maturity.

Everyone Gets Something

According to the world system, you have to fight for what you have, nothing is ever fair, someone is always being taken advantage of, and there always seems to be some sort of real or perceived privilege that ensures some are on top and others are pushed to the bottom of life's ladder of success. This dynamic can lead to frustration and even hopelessness. However, in God's Kingdom, everybody gets a significant investment from the Father and is set up for success from the very beginning, regardless of how long you have been working in the proverbial field discussed in Matthew 25. Even if, or maybe especially if, you struggle with the idea that God has invested anything in you, or that you're really an artist, realize God has invested much in you for His Glory, and that you are meant to experience the fullness of abundant life in Him. Everyone in God's Kingdom gets a measure of divine investment, so it's not a matter of wondering if you received anything. Yes, you've been given something! Something is in your hands right now to steward; whether it's your family, a talent, resources, relationships, or ideas, you've been given something. And whether you've been in the field for a few minutes or you've been in there for 30 years, you have received a divine investment from your Creator.

A Generous Investment

The "talent" God has entrusted to you actually belongs to God, and that's a really important distinction. Just to clarify, I'm talking about talents in a very broad sense of whatever God has invested in you. As you start to understand this whole idea of being entrusted with an investment that ultimately belongs to God and is meant for His Glory, you start to get the picture that God wants you to thrive in this thing called life more than you do. Your job is to cooperate with Him, meaning to see and agree, and not try to do this whole thing on your own. If you do try to do this whole thing on your own, you are going to be really tired, really frustrated, and really burned out. Trust me on this one; I've got that t-shirt.

Now, I think it's important to realize what the Bible actually means when it talks about a talent in the story of Matthew 25. Just for context, a denarius was one day of skilled labor back during the time when Jesus told this parable. Comparatively, a talent then was the equivalent of six thousand denarius or sixteen years wages. Now that is a huge amount of money and almost unfathomable for us to think about someone giving to a farmhand! So, when the Master gives the first guy in the story five talents, He was literally given the equivalent of over two lifetimes of salary.

My friend, realize that when God puts something inside of you when He invests something inside of you, it's not just some meaningless thing. He's entrusted you with something of incalculable value that has the capacity to be used by Him to release provision as your life is led by His Spirit.

Investment Based on God-Enabled Ability

In the Matthew 25 parable, it's also clear everyone received talents based on their abilities. That word "abilities" is actually translated from the word "dynamis," which means for the believer, "*power* to achieve by applying the Lord's *inherent abilities* or power through God's ability." Again, the context here is in relying on

God's power, resident in your life through the Holy Spirit, and cooperating with that power to see results happen in line with your unique gifting, calling, and design. You can't just run off and try to make things happen on your own and ask God

to bless your mess. It doesn't work that way.

Authentic humility is always a hallmark of someone who is maturing in God, and yet it's often misunderstood. Humility is not about self-deprecation or denying who you really are, nor is it about walking around quiet as a church mouse, trying not to be noticed out of fear of being perceived as prideful. True humility is about living a life that is fully infused with the presence and power of God, knowing that it's Him who is doing the work in and through your life.

This can often be a struggle for artists because we see much of what we do creatively as "our work." Of course, we work, we invest, and we enjoy what we create, but that's not what defines us. It's part of our design in the Kingdom, but it's not who we are. People who struggle with pride, creative or otherwise, usually have this concept mixed up, believing that what they do defines who they are, and when that is jeopardized, big problems arise. The Father's best for us is that we embrace our relationship with Christ and enjoy our Kingdom assignment as we flow in His power and might.

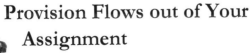

Provision Flows out of Your Assignment

We also see provision flowing to these three

men in line with their assignment. They were working in the master's field, and because of that assignment, they were given everything they needed to accomplish their assignment based on their measure of ability. The provision wasn't given to people walking by the field, or even those who were needy. It was given to those who were already on assignment.

Friend, if you are struggling with finances as a creative person, one big reason may be that you're chasing money from ideas, pursuits, and places God never intended for you. Instead of stopping the train of life for a moment and asking the Lord whether or not your plans are actually part of His design for your life, are you just continuing to do your own thing in hopes for God's mercy and few crumbs from His table? Listen that is not God's best for you! You were designed for more! God has a beautiful way for you to receive provision for everything you need in this life. Let me share that with you.

I learned years ago from one of my favorite Bible teachers, Gary Keesee, that God has designed us to harvest our provision by revelation in the context of our assignment in the Kingdom. Understanding that simple concept absolutely changed the very course of my life. When you understand that you don't have to go out and chase money to make it in this life, things begin to change.

Just the other day I reconnected with a friend of mine in Australia who's been on this journey of understanding her Kingdom assignment and how provision flows within her calling. Here's part of her story:

> "When I prayed for the Lord to give me an idea, I started to think of setting up a music school. I had done this in previous years, and I enjoyed it, but it was still 'money for time.' It would require a lot of my time, a lot of one on one with people, and setting it up from home which meant it would disrupt our family life as we had students streaming in on a constant basis. Now, it wasn't a BAD idea, it would certainly financially provide for us, but it would take up a lot of time, and I would most likely have to cut down how I served ministry-wise. So this idea, although it seemed the most profitable and practical, was also going take the biggest chunk of our time. For me to hear what God was saying, I had to change my mindset.
>
> When the idea finally came, and I knew it was the Lord, it was so different than what I expected. He said, "Roma, how about creating online courses?" At first, I laughed. I had no skills to do that or even the confidence to do it. Now, two years on and 16,000 students later, it has been a transformational idea that has allowed me to minister to more people than I could ever have imagined (including in my sleep)! And guess what? I'm more creative than I have ever been!"

Roma Waterman, www.RomaWaterman.com

You Can't Serve Two Masters

Remember, Jesus said in Matthew 6:24 that we can't serve two masters because we end up loving one and hating the other. The mammon system of this world is one we're all familiar with. It's where you go trade time for money, chase money in any form, hoard money, or fear the lack of money. In this system, folks live from paycheck to paycheck while praying for a windfall or the winning lottery ticket just so they can check out of the money rat race.

Gary Keesee said in his book, *Fixing the Money Thing*:

> *"Jesus is unequivocally saying that there are two systems in this life, two kingdoms and you can't serve both at the same time. You'll serve the master whom you trust the most to meet your needs. It doesn't matter how much you jump and shout in church when you've got to make a significant life decision. You'll always default to the one master you consider most capable of meeting your needs."*

He goes on to talk about how Adam's rebellion from God caused him to forfeit God's ability to provide for him, instantly causing him to be a survivalist. "From that moment on, his entire life became consumed with the quest for provision. Every thought he had would be filtered through the finding-provision mindset. When Adam lost his provision, it was not the only thing he lost. You see, when Adam lost his provision, he lost vision for his life. His vision became one of just surviving each day – running after money, or hoarding money he had."

This survivalist mindset is even prevalent in the church! We just over-spiritualize it and call it a Christian work ethic. We value and esteem people who have gone out there and made it happen by the sweat of their brow believing that everything in life has to come through hard labor. I want to tell you there's another way, my friend, that is grounded in cooperating with the Holy Spirit and flowing in divine favor rather than making it by your own power. You can either do life like everyone else does and get what everyone else has, or you can do things God's way and get all that God has for you. Let me explain.

In the Kingdom, everything flows out of our identity with the Father. Nothing is separate from Him, and in His Kingdom, you've been given an assignment based on your unique design. As you press into Him, understanding who you are in Him and what He's called you to, you can trust that He is going to bring the finances, the relationships, the strategies, and the resources to you at the right time in order for you to walk out your assignment. The more faithful you are to that process, the more you'll grow in maturity in the Kingdom.

Now don't get mad and think, "Matt said I am living in compromise, so I am going to go quit my job tomorrow!" You know if you do, your spouse is going to be calling to have a talk with me, but that's not what I am saying here. There is always a bridge from wherever you are now to wherever God is taking you. I didn't immediately step into what I am doing now overnight. It's taken me years to be able to walk fully in what I am doing now, where my income is based primarily on artwork, writing, speaking, and mentoring. It's taken a process with lots of twists and turns, but as I've tried my best to be faithful with a little, he's making me ruler of much.

As I write this, I'm thinking of a recent testimony from one of the artists who's in my mentoring group as she shared about the process of breakthrough in her life. She wrote:

"My breakthrough has been a series of little breakthroughs rather than one big one. Like a chick cracking her shell. Those "pecks" include: Embracing my call, celebrating my Jesus, rejoicing with others and not having to compare, building habits of long-haul consistency, building a consistent body of work to show and trusting that still small voice for my personal pace. Welcoming newcomers (to the mentoring group) and realizing how much I've already gleaned when I see them ask the same questions I started with. Cheering them on! Having those ahead of me cheering me on! Learning to follow the breadcrumbs on the marketing trail - even if they lead through some uphill trails of grubby hard work. Still breaking through and not giving up!" L. Crouch

My friend, He has the same thing for you! A wonderful, winding process onward and upward to all He's promised! As you are faithful and attuned to what God is doing in your life, He will begin to show you the bridge of how to walk into whatever He ultimately has for you. If that's moving from being a hobbyist or part-time artist to one that sells your work full-time as a vocation, then wonderful! As you learn to hear His voice and follow His lead, the bridge will begin to form in front of you. Remember, in Christ; there is an unlimited abundance of resources. Suffice to say; money should be the very least of your worries because money is not the issue. The question is, are you aligning with a design that God has for you and trusting Him in the process?

Oh Ye of Little Faith

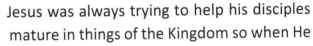

Jesus was always trying to help his disciples mature in things of the Kingdom so when He was gone; they could operate in its fullness. In fact, when you look at the totality of the Biblical narrative, you see the Father continuously concerned with helping His people step into the fullness of who He created them to be, or in other words, to come into maturity. Nowhere is this dynamic more obvious than in the book of Matthew, chapters 6 through 17. Within these chapters are five passages I'd like to draw your attention to because they all have something very unique in common. Here are the passages:

- Matthew 6:30 – Jesus talks about faith for provision
- Matthew 8:26 – Jesus talks about faith for protection
- Matthew 14:31 – Jesus talks about faith for taking risks
- Matthew 16:8 – Jesus again talks about faith for provision
- Matthew 17:20 – Jesus talks about faith for working miracles

In each of the passages above, Jesus addresses those to whom He's speaking as "ye of little faith." Why is that so important with regards to maturity, you might ask? Because God's Word says in Hebrews 11:6, "Without faith it is impossible to please

God." (NIV) You see, faith is the currency of the Kingdom. Without it, no transaction happens, and with it, anything is possible. If Heaven is going to invade the earth through God's people, people just like you and me, then faith is how it will happen. Faith literally opens the door for God to move in and through your life.

Now, these five passages of scripture where Jesus uses the phrase "you of little faith" address a few key areas in your journey to maturity in God's Kingdom, including the provision, protection, and the power available to you through your relationship with Christ. These three areas are also the same exact areas that Jesus was tempted with when He was in the wilderness after He was baptized by John the Baptist. Any time a concept is repeated in God's Word, it's important you pay close attention. This is one of those times.

You see, my friend, unless you are actively growing in maturity within these three areas, how God provides for you, protects you, and works through you in His Kingdom, you'll never walk in the fullness of what He has planned for you. Learning to overcome the work of the enemy in your life in these three specific areas, through the strength of your renewed mind as empowered by the Holy Spirit, is non-negotiable. You either mature or stagnate. You either grow or die. You either produce fruit, or you are a weed. There's no middle ground.

Growing in Wisdom & Stature

In Luke 2:52 it says, "Jesus grew in wisdom and

in stature, and in favor with God and man." (NIV) I love this description because again, it shows Jesus is our example as we grow in the Kingdom and how we should be modeling ourselves after Him. If we're maturing like Jesus did, then we're growing in wisdom, knowing what to do, how to do, and doing it with favor from both God and man. The connotation of the word "favor" means to be inclined toward or leaning towards to share benefits. Those are a couple of key markers you can look for and welcome into your life as you continue to grow in stewardship with what God is doing in your life. It's normal to expect wisdom to flood your life. It's normal to expect favor, blessing, and situations where people lean into you with special benefits. I know, it sounds too good to be true, but friend, this is normal Christianity in the Kingdom.

God's investment in your life is not just about you but about His nature and His glory being revealed and released in the earth through us as his sons and daughters. The revival the church is praying for and that the world so desperately needs is inextricably tied to us. The world is crying out for God's sons and daughters to stand up and walk in the fullness of who He's created us to be. He will be revealed, and His nature released, in a myriad of different ways as we just live the life that He has called us to live. When we do that, the nature of God through our lives is a beautiful breeze across the earth, a sweet-smelling incense before Him, and a balm to others.

Diamonds in Lumps of Coal

My friend Ray HughEs always says that God

gives us diamonds in lumps of coal. I love that because it's such a perfect metaphor for how God works. When God reveals something to you, it rarely comes floating down from heaven in its finished form. I wrote extensively about this topic in my book, *Creativity According to the Kingdom,* but suffice it to say, when the Father releases revelation, He's giving you the opportunity and the authority to begin to move out toward the revelation. As you move and listen and look expectantly for the Holy spirit to intersect your path, you start picking up on the clues of what's God is doing. Make sense? Remember, God's Word teaches us in Proverbs 25:2, that it's the glory of God to conceal a matter, and the glory of kings to search it out.

Filled & Skilled

Lastly, growth in the Kingdom of God happens when you lean in into being both filled and skilled. Now if you have ever been to one of our Gathering of Artisans conferences or are a part of my Created to Thrive Artist Mentoring Program, you've probably heard me talk about being filled and skilled out of the story of Bezalel in Exodus 31. I talk about this concept everywhere I go, because I believe it to be one of the foundational concepts in God's Kingdom, not just for artists, but for every person wanting to thrive in all God has for him. It is not just enough to be filled with the Spirit and sit around, enjoying the glory of His presence. As wonderful and vital as that is in our life, it should lead us out of our comfort zones and ourselves. As we grow in His presence, we must also lean into skill development, because that enlarges our capacity to be carriers of His presence. Skill and mastery enable us to steward well the gifts, talents, callings, and opportunities that God gives us. Without a beautiful balance, we run around in circles either full of passion but lacking skill or extremely skilled with no life. It's a collaboration between God and man, and in no way does that downgrade the supernatural component of how God works in our life.

If you're like me, you've probably had many times in your life when you asked, "God, can't you just supernaturally download this thing to me so I can get on with it?" And of course, He could absolutely do that, but more than likely it's going to happen the way I am describing in this book. Not because God is mad or doesn't love you, but because He's all about the process of walking with us on the journey. He has invested something in you, and He wants to lead, guide, and inspire you with opportunities every day of your life so that you come to know the beauty and adventure of walking with Him! As you faithfully continue on that journey, increase and fruitfulness will be yours. That's just how the Kingdom works.

To take your learning deeper, check out my free resource, 29 Habits of All Thriving Artists, at:

www.MattTommeyMentoring.*com/cttfree

For Such A Time As This

And who knows but that you have come to your royal position for such a time as this." Esther 4:14 NIV

I was on Facebook just the other day reading a post from one of the artists from my Created to Thrive Artist Mentoring program, Dionne. She was sharing a challenging time from her own journey of answering God's call on her life as an artist. It was evidently a time in her life where she was painting a lot but unfortunately not selling a lot, and as with many artists, she began to take this lack of sales personally. The enemy started to use it as a place of discouragement in her life, even causing her to question her calling as a creative. Sound familiar?

Here's the exciting part of the story, she didn't stay there! Instead of wallowing in self-pity, she turned and asked the Lord to show her His truth about what she was feeling and the truth about her calling. He responded by reminding of her calling to display His Glory through her creative expression and how that didn't necessarily mean creating work with a Biblical theme or metaphor. Rather, He began to reinforce the fact that she was displaying His Glory simply by answering the call to co-create with Him.

My friend that is such a foundational truth in God's Kingdom! I've always said that God cares more that you create with Him than what you create for Him. It's about aligning with your unique design and learning to flow with that design as a conduit for releasing the power of His Kingdom! It's about connecting with something that's so much bigger than yourself, your desires, and your art. It's about stepping into His eternal story because that's the place where you'll both experience abundant life and be used by Him to offer that same abundant life to others. It's about embracing your unique design for such a time as this!

The Story of Esther

I love the story of Esther. In fact, if you've never taken the time to read the book of Esther, I'd encourage you to. It's a short but powerful story, especially verse 4:14, where it says, "For if you remain silent in this time, relief and deliverance for the Jews will arise from another place, but you and your father's family will perish. And who knows but that you have come to your royal position for such a time as this." (NIV)

If you don't know who Esther was, she was this beautiful young Jewish woman who basically was chosen to marry King Xerxes after a long selection process. In fact, she ended up going through twelve months of preparation before ever meeting the king. This is such a wonderful picture of how preparation in life is so vital in fulfilling God's ultimate purposes for your life. The whole story is about Esther's divine setup to be used by God in the household of the king to execute the will of God in that particular circumstance. On the surface, however, she seemed most unqualified for the task.

Calling & Qualification

It's rare for anyone to automatically step into the fullness of who God has called him to be without any preparation. Take Jesus, for example. He lived for thirty years before stepping into just three years of public ministry. Moses was the same way. Look at the example of Bezelel in Exodus 31. Although we don't have direct word on this, I surmise from the way I see God work throughout His Word in the lives of others that Bezelel had lived, worked, and been faithful in his calling right up until the time he was released into the fullness of what he was called to do in building the tabernacle. It's just the way things work in the Kingdom.

Henry Blackaby, the author of *Experiencing God,* said, "The reality is that the Lord never calls the qualified; He qualifies the called." This is such an appropriate word, especially as you consider the story of Esther. Even though she went through a season of intense preparation and was in the king's court, she was still a very young and unprepared woman. You've probably felt the same way from time to time in your own life, in the right place to make a difference but feeling completely unprepared.

You see, all children of God are called, and as we respond to the call, God begins to direct our steps by His Spirit. I always jokingly say that God directs our steps, not our standing still! Of course, you must always build time into the normal rhythm of life to wait on the Lord and allow Him to renew your strength, but it's equally vital to get up and let Him direct your steps based on what He's just shown you. That's how it works. Otherwise, you end up in one extreme or another; soaking in His presence and never acting on the revelation you receive or living life out of your own strength with little regard for the leadership of the Holy Spirit. Neither of those reflects God's best.

The reality is that we are qualified and matured and become ruler over much as we faithfully walk out our calling over time. When God created you, He called you, marked you, and designed a specific purpose for your life. You have a purpose in Him that was designed before the very foundation of the earth, and at some point in your life, you will begin to resonate and agree with that calling. Just because I might have felt called at twelve years old that God was going to use me in ministry in some way, didn't mean I was qualified. I might have been called, but I wasn't qualified. As you consider the ultimate vision and direction for your life, realize that there is a divine calling and investment already in place in your life. You don't have to beg God to give you something that's already there! It's simply a matter of connecting with what He's placed inside of you through the Kingdom, so you can resonate with His frequency in your life.

No matter what your current situation looks like, the plan and purpose for your life is going to be revealed as you trust and seek Him in the process. Don't be deceived into thinking that somehow the complete manuscript of your life is just going to float down from the portals of heaven, ready for you to act on with precision. Yes, just like Esther, your life is based on the design and promise of God in your life, but it's also determined by how you respond to that design through the choices you make. No matter what life looks like currently, you can trust that as you collaborate with the Holy Spirit, He is going to continue to reveal the plan and purpose for your life.

Transformed to Release Transformation

God is always strategically positioning sons and daughters into places of influence within our culture, almost like chess pieces. He does this not only for His Glory and for His purposes but also that you would be refined and live the abundant life He designed for you. How beautiful, that God would use us to restore and establish His Kingdom in the earth by being fruitful, multiplying, and subduing the earth. This is what restoration of the Kingdom looks like. We are changed to be agents of change, restored to be agents of restoration, reconciled to be ministers of reconciliation, filled with His life to be conduits of the same.

At the beginning of the Genesis story of creation, there's a wonderful picture painted for us to understand how creation happened. It describes an environment that was dark, chaotic, and void. In the middle of that environment, the Bible said that the Spirit of God hovered, and He said let there be light. But I don't believe God was just saying, "Turn on the lights." There seems to be much more to the story.

In John 1:1, the Bible says: "In the beginning was the Word, the Word was with God, the Word was God." (NIV) Verse 4 goes on to say, "In Him was life and the life was the light of men." (ESV) Did you catch that? In God, there is both the life and light; his nature is both life and light. I believe when God said, "Let there be light" in Genesis, He was saying something deeper like, "Let there be a release of my nature, or, "Let the light of my nature invade this environment that is dark, chaotic, and void." When God declared the light of His very nature to be released, all of a sudden everything was transformed! My friend, when God shows up, life as we know it is transformed.

So, what does this have to do with you? Everything! As His

sons and daughters who have been brought back into relationship with Him through Jesus, we are image bearers, light bearers, and by the authority that has been given to us through Jesus, we have the opportunity to release His light and life through our life, and yes, even our creative expression! When the Holy Spirit moves through us, through our lives, and through our art, we can expect that transformation will follow, because when the nature of God shows up on the scene, things change!

I recently had the privilege of being asked to create a nine-foot-wide sculpture for a new cancer center here in western North Carolina. As I was creating it, the Lord told me to call it "Nested in Arms of Grace." I really enjoyed making the piece and seeing it unveiled before hundreds of people at the grand opening of the center, but that's not the end of the story! I believe it's going to be more than just a beautiful piece of art. I believe people who view the piece as they are going in for cancer treatments are going to have an encounter with God's presence, and I am waiting for the testimonies to come in! Why not? Can you imagine that phone call? "Uh is this Matt? Well, I was at the cancer center today, and I saw your piece hanging on the wall. All of a sudden my body began to tremble, something came over me, and my doctor just confirmed that I'd been completely healed of cancer!" Why not?

Listen, if God can speak truth through a donkey, use Moses' stuttering tongue, Abraham who doubted him, and the disciples who denied Him after walking with Him day by day, then why not you and me? The whole point of God placing me in situations of influence is not just for my benefit but to release His Kingdom! The same is absolutely true for you, but there needs to be an expectation in your heart for those things to start manifesting. As you begin to receive those things that God has for you, start actively looking for the manifestation of His Kingdom in your life. Then, start making room for it. That's part of the Kingdom package, getting to live life to the fullest!

Why Doesn't God Just Do It?

People often wonder why God doesn't just show up and fix everything on the earth. I've wondered that myself, but it's not because He can't or doesn't want to. It's certainly not because He's a distant being who is unconcerned with the triviality of life on earth. No, it's because He's given that authority and opportunity to His children; He's given it to you and me. Listen, this is huge! Sure, God could do anything He wanted at any time He wanted, but He has chosen to move through us. He knows that involves us in the excitement and adventure of advancing His Ever-expanding Kingdom.

Remember, when God shows you something, whether it's an idea for your business, your art, or anything you're passionate about, rarely does that come to you in a finished form. I mean, think about it! With ideas and promptings that come from the Spirit, God is giving you the opportunity and authority to begin to walk in that direction and search out the secrets He has just for you!

You know, when God gave me the burden to raise up an army of artists, I didn't get a complete game plan with step-by-step instructions. I've had to learn to lean into His voice, course correct along the way, and trust Him on the journey. I never in a million years would have been able to conceive all that God has poured out in my life in just these few short years since 2009, and I can't imagine what's on the horizon. That's the adventure; that's living life abundantly!

When I started sensing the creative direction to create sculptural works in branches that resembled nests, pods, and rocks, it wasn't a clean, easy process. For a couple of years, I heard in my spirit: "Elevate the basket," and I was like, "What in the world does that mean?" I didn't know if it that was metaphorical, spiritual, or actual elevation. So, I started experimenting by placing baskets on pedestals and on rocks. I was placing baskets on anything that would sit still, but it just wasn't working. It felt awkward. Then, I was drawn to branches and early Japanese ikebana baskets. Immediately, I began to resonate with this creative direction and as I pressed in more, guess what? My work began to evolve quickly, and my clients began resonating with my work too, resulting in significantly increased sales.

Are you starting to see how this works? I didn't get the full revelation when I got the initial inspiration. I received inspiration in a moment that continues to result in the revelation unfolding as I faithfully pursue the process. As I do, faith rises, and I know God is leading me. The more I walk in this journey with Him, the more confident I am of His leadership and pleasure.

What's In Your Hand?

Start asking the Lord to show you what's in your hand. What do you see? What burdens your heart? What are you passionate about? Many times, it's the things that are a part of your natural design. God wants to move through your life right now. However, if you are waiting for the exact blueprint and the perfect timing to get started, you'll become paralyzed by good intentions. Listen to His voice, watch as He awakens your desires, commit your ways to the Lord, and start walking. He's right there with you, and I promise you, the Father wants you to step into the fullness of your purpose more than you do!

Don't ever allow fear of making a mistake be a paralyzing factor in your walk with the Lord. As you live secure in His love, be free to step up and do something that's scary. Get in the studio and create something ugly! Remember, most people have to create a lot of ugly before they get to the beautiful. Start stepping out in the authority and opportunity He gives you, then all of a sudden your influence will start to grow. Over time, your vision will become clearer, and that's kind of how the journey unfolds.

The Blooming of Destiny

The sense of divine destiny you long for in your life will bloom like a beautiful flower as you start to embrace the fact that you are fully equipped to be part of a story that's bigger than just you. I've already shared a lot on the power of renewing your mind in earlier chapters, but I want to emphasize this again. Second Peter 2 teaches that you've been given everything you need for life in godliness. You are not a slave, you're a son or daughter, and you surely don't have to beg God for anything. According to God's Word, everything you need is already yours in the Kingdom that lives inside of you right now. The issue is not for you to beg God, saying, "Oh God, things are so bad, and I'm so bad too, but I need this or that just to make it through today. Please have mercy on me, an old sinner." No way!! It's time for faith to arise as you begin to pray, "Father, I thank you today that I aligned with you in such a way that I can receive in fullness what you already gave to me in your Kingdom. I am so happy and thankful now that I have everything I need for life and godliness, and I receive it now by faith. Thank you, that you're a good Father who loves me, provides for me, cares for me, and has plans to prosper me and to give me a hope and a future!"

Praying Toward Vision

Do you see how that works? I call it praying toward vision, not praying out of need. I wish I could sit down with you right now, open up your mind, and pour this in because it's that important. Whatever you focus on grows and gets magnified in your life. What do you want to grow: thoughts and feelings of fear, lack, shame, and control, or thoughts and feelings of faith, provision, abundance, purpose, and confidence in the Lord? When you approach the Lord boldly, in gratefulness, receiving what He has for you, it will literally begin to drive out that lesser, fear-based thinking and completely renew your mind. Hallelujah!

Ambassador On Assignment

As a child of God, you are already commissioned as His ambassador on the earth to release his power and his nature for such a time as this. You have a divine purpose and the divine provision you need to pursue your divine assignment with divine authority. Realize, ambassadors have the authority to make a change in the name of the one who sent them.

Right now, as I write this in America, we have just come through a historic election, and the new President is in the process of choosing a new Secretary of State and other Cabinet members. Whoever is selected as Secretary of State will travel around the world to hundreds of countries as a primary ambassador of the President. When he says something to another world leader, it will effect change in that country, or in the relationship, the U.S. has with that country, based on what is said. The President doesn't have to go. He simply sends his ambassador, because he has given the ambassador all the authority he needs to do the job as desired by the President. Friend, realize you've been sent as well, but by one much greater than any political leader. You've been called, commissioned, and sent by the King of Kings to be an ambassador of His Kingdom in the earth.

What you are doing in the creative realm is not just art for art's sake; you're literally creating these Holy Ghost intersection points, these outposts in the world, and these relationships where God then has access to use us in what we do creatively to release transformation in and through us. This is normal Christianity; this can happen every day of your life.

Time with Jesus

Thriving in your divine design requires regular time alone with the Lord to hear his voice, to discern your direction, and to deepen your relationship with Him. It's the habits of your life that create space for God to move, and it's the habits you create which will enlarge your capacity to be used by Him. Almost every morning, I spend 20 to 30 minutes in my favorite chair just taking time to drink my coffee, journal, pray, meditate on His promises, say my affirmations, and visualize my day with the Holy Spirit. It's just a habit I've formed in my life, but the fruit this habit has produced is overwhelming. So much of what the Lord shows me happens during those special times with Him.

It Requires Bravery

It's not enough, however, to just sit and receive. If you spend time with Jesus, He'll always draw you out of your comfort zone and into the marketplace of life. Faith requires getting up and walking it out.   Life doesn't just happen on autopilot. It requires searching and knocking and trying and failing. For artists, it requires creating a lot of ugly things, and all of this requires risk. You know, that's what the Kingdom of God is about: risking your reputation, thoughts, and desires in order to experience His life through you. The Kingdom suffers violence, and the violent take it by force.

This kind of living also requires bravery in the face of everything that wants to destroy you, but that's the way Kingdom advances. That's the way you step into the fullness of who God has called you to be, but you can't do that unless you deal with your identity issues, unhealthy mindsets, thought life, and your inner paradigm. All of those systems need to be working inside of you in order for that Spirit-led bravery to kick in at maximum capacity.

Your North Star

As you begin walking bravely through this life, your Kingdom purpose and your divine design essentially become your north star. They become your guiding beacon and measuring stick by which everything else in your life gets evaluated. Creative people are usually good at a lot of different things. There are a lot of things that you might be good at, but it doesn't mean that these are the things you're supposed to be doing. You have to be able to say no to the "wrong things" in order to say yes to the "right things." How do you know the right things from the wrong things, you might ask? You evaluate them in light of where God has placed you, how He's designed you, and the vision He's given you for your life.

For example, I know right now in this season of my life I'm a dad, a husband, an artist, and a father to artists around the world. Those are the four things that I do, and I focus almost exclusively on those four areas, making decisions accordingly. Anything that I give time, resources, or attention to in my life has to fall within one of those four categories, or I don't do it. Because of that practice, I'm able to be extremely effective in what I do while not wasting time on ancillary activities that don't have anything to do with who God's called me to be. I hope this is making sense to you.

Just to give you a real-life example, one of the things that Tanya and I really felt in this season of our family life is that I needed to be investing significant time with our son Cameron, who is awesome by the way! He's a great kid, and it's that time of life where he's walking through all the challenges of adolescence. I want to be there for him and develop a strong bond during this time, so he stays strong.

Now, ever since I moved to Asheville, I've hosted a weekly small group of artists in my studio. I was beginning to feel like that season was coming to a close, and instead of freaking out about it or having a bunch of shame, I began actively seeking the Lord on what was next. Instead of trying to keep it going out of religious obligation, I trusted that as God closed this door, He was opening another. I used the transition time to take a breather and recalibrate. Now I take Cameron to Boy Scouts on Monday nights.

You know some people would say, "Matt, God's called you to the nations, you should be going to the nations, and blah, blah, blah..." Yes, that's true, but God didn't call me to do that and lose my family. You know, I can't travel all the time and be the father, husband, and artist I know God's called me to be. That's one of the main reasons I write books and have my online artist program, Created to Thrive. I am literally able to touch thousands upon thousands of artists in a significant way all while being true to where God has me right now in this season of my life. When you begin to make the tough decisions that craft your life around your divine design, all of a sudden you'll start to see things flow together with great harmony. There will be supernatural momentum in your life as opposed to feeling like you're burned out on every end.

One of my favorite quotes is by Arthur Wallis, one of the fathers of the charismatic movement in England, who once said, "If you would do the best with your life, find out what God is doing in your generation and throw yourself wholly into it."

Thriving in God's Kingdom is not about you creating the momentum but rather flowing with the momentum that God has already created in your life and in this generation, then aligning yourself with that, so you that literally become a display of His Glory.

Moving from Hobby to Pro

Whatever you do, work at it with all your heart, as working for the Lord
Colossians 3:23

One of the things I never had on my journey was a roadmap. "Where do I go? What's the next thing I need to do? What should I focus on to help me grow?" These are questions the Lord has always been so faithful to show me answers for, and yet, I've found over the years that there are some concrete steps everyone must take on this journey from surviving to thriving as an artist. I want to share those with you in this chapter.

Rather than thinking of these as ordered steps, I want you to see this chapter as a collection of signposts along your journey. When you see these, you'll know you are heading in the right direction, because rarely do they come in the same order for anyone.

In addition, for all of you who might have skipped through to this chapter saying, "I just want to know what to do," please go back to the beginning! All the practical tips and tricks in the world won't do anything for you if you are holding onto an unhealthy belief system and have a weak spiritual connection to the Lord and the plans He has for you. That is the whole point of this book: to help you understand who you really are, so you can cultivate that over time, and when you start to make real changes, as led by the Spirit of God and the mentors in your life, they are able to stick over the long haul. Now that we're on the same page let's jump in!

As you know by now, I make my living as a full-time vocational artist, speaker, author, and leader of an online artist mentoring community. Because of that dynamic, I get asked one question a lot in almost every situation I find myself. It goes something like this: "I'm a (fill in the blank) artist, and I want to start selling my work (or start making money, start thriving, etc.), but I just can't seem to choose a direction. I like everything. What should I do?"

Questions like this encapsulate the dilemma that many emerging artists face. "How do I move from being a hobbyist to a more serious part-time or full-time artist?" It's a big frustration that keeps many people, maybe even you, up at night, causing confusion and even anxiety about their purpose in life. However, it doesn't have to be that way.

I want to compare and contrast the way hobbyists approach their art practice versus the way professional artists approach theirs. This is not to say that all hobbyists are immature or that all professionals have 'made it.' However, in my experience in working with artists, and from my own journey, these attributes are true for many. Hopefully, this comparison will give you some insight into where you are now and how to start moving towards being a thriving artist!

First of all, let's define the terms hobbyist, emerging, professional, and thriving artist. As I've reflected on my own journey and the journeys of the literally hundreds of artists who are a part of my Created to Thrive Artist Mentoring program, I now understand there are basic stages artists goes through on their journey of creativity. Most artists stop somewhere along the way, but for those who refuse to give up, they reap the rewards of perseverance.

Hobbyist

All artists start here, creating from a place of passion, connection, and expression. The focus for the hobbyists is creating for their own enjoyment. Hobbyists pursue their art at their leisure and don't always have a dedicated space to create. Hobbyists enjoy the freedom of creating when inspiration strikes, once a week, a couple of times a month, or even a few times a year. They often continue to create because of the spiritual connection they feel when creating.

The main challenges facing these artists include frustration with lack of skill, dedicating time to create, connecting with other creatives for community and encouragement, and beliefs surrounding their own identity as artists. They might want more from their art, but for a variety of reasons, including time management, lack of focus, or simply being overwhelmed with life, it never seems to happen.

Emerging Artist

After creating for some time as a hobbyist, artists who are emerging begin to develop a passion for a more focused pursuit of their art. They start getting serious about developing more skill, spending more time on their artistic development, and selling their work to others. Emerging artists are intentional about developing the basics of their art business, including things like a website, printed materials, professional photography, having dedicated studio space, and applying for shows. As you can see, their art has become important enough to be a main focus of their time, attention, and resources.

Key challenges facing emerging artists include renewing their mind to align with God's Word rather than their own experience or beliefs, building healthy relationships with other artists who are on the same journey, and balancing time to create with relationships and administrative tasks required to launch an art business. This is where many artists give up, because it's in this phase of development that things get very real, very quickly. In fact, many emerging artists stay here for years because they don't understand how to make all these moving parts work together.

Professional Artist

Artists who do start to find balance and momentum with their art, and all the moving parts required to support a professional art career, move into the professional phase of life after several years of honing their skills and developing their unique creative voice. These artists usually has a dedicated studio space, spend time creating on a daily basis, and regularly pursue selling their work via social networks, shows, commissions, and other venues. Their friends and colleagues recognize them as seasoned professionals, seriously pursuing their creative expression. They have developed their own unique marketing brand and work to connect with those who connect with their creative voice via their website, social media, printed media, and referrals.

The main challenges facing professional artists include cultivating fresh creativity while building upon the success they've experienced, asking for help from professionals in order to grow their businesses to the next level, cash flow, and time management. As professional artists experience success, it's even more important for them to keep their life and art centered in a vital relationship with Jesus. I've found the biggest barrier to my own connection with the Lord can be success. Now, that doesn't mean God doesn't want you to succeed. It's just that our success should always be viewed in the context of our relationship with Him and our role in the Kingdom!

Thriving Artist

Over time, as an artist experiences real flow in his life, he looks around and says, "Wow, I'm living the dream!" He has moved from hobbyist to emerging artist, to professional artist, and is now thriving in his chosen creative pursuits. Thriving artists create what they love in a dedicated studio space while selling their work for top dollar to clients who seek it out. Their lives are marked by creative fulfillment, financial abundance, meaningful relationships, and deep spiritual connection. These artists have developed a niche of clients who authentically connect with them and their work as reflected by their willingness to purchase and refer them to their circle of influence.

The main challenges facing these artists include balancing time with family and friends versus time given to their business and art pursuits, cultivating a thriving relationship with the Holy Spirit, and taking time to give back to others along the journey who need to know what they've learned over the years.

My friend, no matter where you are on your journey as an artist, God wants to use you for His Glory in order to release His Life and Light into the world. You can be the thriving artist God designed you to be if you're willing to start aligning with Him.

Signposts of Thriving

When I think about what it has taken for me to become a full-time thriving vocational artist, I think about nine different categories: Time Management, Artistic Style, Inspiration, Growth, Spiritual Connection, Sales, Business, Success, and Approach. Each one of these categories is vital to your success as you move from hobbyist to thriving. Let's see why, as I compare and contrast each of these in the context of some of the biggest questions I get from artists who want to really start thriving.

"How do I balance the demands of my life while pursuing my art?"

This question is probably the biggest question I get from hobbyists and emerging artists because they've not yet figured out how to manage their time and resources. They procrastinate before taking steps and only pursue their art when they feel they have time to spare as a pastime or opportunity for personal enjoyment. However, this dilemma of wanting more but not being able to see it manifest in their life is more than just a bother, it's a huge frustration and seems to be the most significant hurdle for these artists to get over.

I always say the same thing to artists who are struggling with time management issues; you don't have a time management problem, you have a priorities problem. You see, whatever you see as important in your life, you will give time, attention, and resources toward. That's human nature. Artists who struggle with time management, especially with regard to allowing other people to dictate how their time is spent, have not yet learned to value themselves and their artistic gifting as part of their role in God's Kingdom. For them, because of the way they view themselves, their giftings, and God, it's just not important enough to fight for.

Artists who are thriving understand who they are in Christ and what God's called them to do as an artist in the Kingdom. They take actionable steps toward their goals and don't sit around waiting for total clarity in every situation before stepping out in faith. Thriving artists prioritize regular studio, skill development, and inspiration time as important parts of their routine and protect that time as valuable.

Lastly, with regard to time management, I see thriving artists in relationships with friends and family who respect their work and calling as an artist. More than likely, these artists have talked to the ones they love about their work as an artist and developed a mutual respect. It's not that these artists are shirking their responsibilities in other areas of life. No! On the contrary, the more focused they are on their art and the Lord's leading in that area, the more fulfilled and effective they will be in all areas of life. Having friends and family who are supportive and understanding of this dynamic is key to being a healthy artist.

If you struggle in this area, I want to give you two practical tips. First, in conjunction with developing a vision board, revisit where it is you're going in your life, and then make sure your schedule supports that new direction. You can't grow and thrive in your creative gifting without making it a priority by giving it the time, resources, and attention it needs to grow. Secondly, once you've done that, gather the ones you love and share this new direction with them. Remember, you're not asking for permission, you're letting them know about a change that's happening in your life and your desire to have their support. Once you do that, you'll start to feel a huge sense of momentum.

"How do I develop my own unique artistic style that's recognizable in the marketplace?"

When starting our artistic journey, most of us begin to experiment with various mediums, styles, and expressions. You might take classes and try all sorts of ideas before you feel like you find your creative direction. That's the fun of being a hobbyist and emerging artist; you get to play, create, and experiment. Otherwise, you'll never know what artistic mediums and processes resonate with you.

The problem arises when artists want to enter the marketplace and see their art become more than just a hobby but never leave this phase of creative discovery and experimentation. As they continue to bounce from medium to medium, process to process, style to style, they never develop a cohesive voice in their work. They start feeling like jacks-of-all-trades while being a masters-of-none.

If you want to be an artist who is able to thrive in the marketplace, meaning you create and actively sell easily recognizable works you love for a living wage or more, you'll have to work hard to develop a cohesive artistic voice within your chosen medium. Obviously, to do that, you have to develop a mastery of the skills needed within your chosen medium to express yourself with excellence. You'll also need to listen closely to those who are responding to your work. As you create and continue to experiment with your chosen style, medium, and process, you'll start to see a cohesive voice emerge.

One of the things I've done over the years that has resulted in a very cohesive, strong creative voice in my work is to limit my palette of materials. I decided long ago, because of my connection with the natural world, that I would primarily use materials that were harvested in my local area. Consequently, I ended up focusing on the use of southern invasive plant species including materials like honeysuckle, kudzu, grapevine, wisteria, and bittersweet, along with a variety of non-invasive, but plentiful, trees and shrubs like tulip, poplar, willow, mountain laurel, and rhododendron. Within those limited materials, I've been able to create unique pieces for over 24 years now, and it's resulted in work that is very distinctive and recognizable in the marketplace. In fact, people often come up to me and ask, "Did you have work at (insert a place)?" When I say yes, they will often respond, "Oh, I just knew that had to be your work!"

Just this morning, I was looking at an artist online whose work as a painter is focused on the exclusive use of ultramarine blue, black, white, and gold leaf. It's striking, recognizable, and not at all limiting to her expression. It's simply the boundary which she's placed around her work which in turn looses her creative freedom. It's kind of like a river. Without the banks, all you have is a flood. Boundaries in your creative expression bring focus and power to your work.

"What can I do to stay inspired creatively?"

Inspiration for artists is like water to a well; without it, all you have is emptiness. If you've ever tried to create without inspiration, you know what I mean. It's like going through the motions with only frustration as your result. Obviously, that's not God's plan for our life! Inspiration, as directed by the Spirit of God, is what brings life to our creative process, but it doesn't just happen automatically.

When we first start creating as hobbyists, we do so sporadically, and that's okay. We see, hear, or feel something that is meaningful to us, and it leads us to create. We get used to needing that immediate inspiration before we create, and it's a beautiful part of how we do art. However, waiting for inspiration can be a crutch and an excuse for procrastination.

I've found in my own life that I have to continuously cultivate and steward inspiration on a regular basis in order to fill, what I call, my creative well. As you walk through your daily life with an ear to what the Lord is saying and revealing, you will continually be inspired. However, you might not always be able to immediately act on that inspiration. The difference between a hobbyist and a thriving artist is how that inspiration is stewarded. Employing daily habits of journaling, sketching, and documenting experiences fill your creative well and allow you to come back to these ideas at a later time. These habits also allow the inspiration to marinate and develop over time, so when you actually do begin creating in the studio, you're doing so with a well-formed idea.

Creative inspirations are like seeds. In and of themselves, they are worthless unless they are planted in good soil and allowed to come to maturity. The tendency for many artists is to paint the seed, use the seed, give away the seed, or even try to sell the seed rather than plant the seed and wait. For seeds to come to maturity, they must be planted in good soil and die before they can give way to life.

You must give inspiration the soil it needs to mature into fruit while dying to your own preconceived notions of what the art should or should not look like based on how you interpreted the seed. Rarely does the seed look like the fruit. Unless you allow the seed to die and then come into maturity, you're probably missing much of what Holy Spirit is actually trying to speak in and through your creative process.

What does this mean practically? Leave room for mystery. Journal your inspirations, record them on Pinterest, create a vision board, meditate on them with the Holy Spirit. Allow them time and space to come to fruition. Otherwise, you're giving away simple seeds or fruit that's not yet ripe. When you release Spirit-birthed fruit, it will both nourish and carry within it seeds of life.

I've also found over the years that inspiration comes as I work. In other words, lack of immediate inspiration is not something that stops me from working. There's a quote from painter Chuck Close in Joe Fig's book, *Inside the Painters Studio*, where he asks Chuck if he had a motto or creed to live by. Chuck responded by saying:

> *"Inspiration is for amateurs — the rest of us just show up and get to work. And the belief that things will grow out of the activity itself and that you will — through work — bump into other possibilities and kick open other doors that you would never have dreamt of if you were just sitting around looking for a great "art idea." And the*

belief that process, in a sense, is liberating and that you don't have to reinvent the wheel every day. Today, you know what you'll do, you could be doing what you were doing yesterday, and tomorrow you are gonna do what you did today, and at least for a certain period of time, you can just work. If you hang in there, you will get somewhere."

I love that because again, it's about process, not product. As we are faithful to show up and do the work, God is faithful to come lead, equip, and inspire us for His Glory.

"How do I grow as an artist? Sometimes I feel creatively stuck!"

Artists who consider their art a hobby usually experience slower growth for a number of different reasons. They can be more impulsive with how they approach their artwork and often lack creative focus, taking shortcuts, creating work they consider "good enough," or they tend to give up easily.

With experience comes a bit of grit, and I find that's what separates people who really grow artistically from those who stagnate. Artists who take their work more seriously from a time, resource, and focus perspective often experience faster growth in their work and career, because they tend to be persistent, desiring excellence, and are always learning. These artists are never satisfied with their last creation, but use it as a stepping stone to what's next on the creative horizon. They are drawn by the Spirit in their artistic process to go from glory to glory. They cultivate the creative well within them, creating from a place of Spirit-led inspiration.

Artists who are serious about growing are also proactive about creating a dedicated studio space in which to work and setting aside time to cultivate a focused studio practice. The artistic process is typically not one that just happens. Rather, it has to be cultivated through time and attention. As you do this, the Holy Spirit shows up in the studio with grace to create. Growth and maturity are the natural results of focused effort enabled by His presence.

"How Do I Create With the Holy Spirit?"

This is one of the most common questions I get from artists of every creative medium, and that's exciting! So many people these days want to see God show up in their creative process. They want to encounter Him as they create, see His Glory shine through what they've created and have others experience real transformation when they encounter their work. I know that's my heart, and I bet it's probably yours as well.

First of all, let me say there's no magic pattern to follow that will all of a sudden make your art "prophetic art," and there's no boundary on what you create in order for it to be used by God. So many artists use the phrases "prophetic art" and "worship painting" interchangeably because painting is the most predominant visual art we see expressed in the church right now. That's wonderful, but worship painting does not encompass the fullness of all prophetic art. Rather, it's one beautiful expression.

Creating with the Holy Spirit is about process, not product. It's about continually cultivating ears to hear, eyes to see, and senses to feel what God is saying and doing within your world and then responding through your chosen creative process. For some people, that's a very intentional process where their art speaks specific messages for specific situations, and for others, like me, it's a much more fluid approach.

For example, as a natural materials sculptor, I create pieces that reflect the beauty of the natural world as I interpret it through my relationship with God. I simply create what I love as I'm inspired, because I believe God put those desires in me, and I sense His pleasure when I'm involved in the creative process. I rarely ask myself, "Is this prophetic or not?" I focus on the process of cultivating my relationship with Him both in and out of my creative expression. The result is that I live a fulfilled life as an artist on assignment in the Kingdom, build relationships with others as the Lord leads, and watch Him do incredible things both through my art and life.

Overthinking or over-spiritualizing the creative process causes your creativity to be stifled, and perfectionism to rise within your heart, which usually leads to shame and procrastination. If you're struggling with whether you're doing it right or not, don't. The best piece of advice I have for you is; don't overcomplicate it. Get with Jesus, learn to hear his voice, and respond authentically through your creative expression. As you do, you'll mature artistically and spiritually while God blows your mind with how He uses you and your work.

"How do I connect with people who will purchase my art for top dollar?"

Let me start by saying, this could be a whole book in itself but there are some key points I want to give you in regards to connecting with clients.

Most artists who are hobbyists or emerging artists experience infrequent or non-existent sales of their work. They end up giving away lots of work to friends, family, and coworkers because they really enjoy creating their work for personal pleasure and their own spiritual processing with the Lord. It's also common for these artists to struggle when trying to place a monetary value on their work because they have no established clientele, presentation, or pricing strategy.

In general, artists who actively sell their work for top dollar on a regular basis do so within an established clientele under a standardized pricing and presentation model. They are confident in the quality and value of their work and are willing to charge a premium. They understand what their clientele responds to within their art and work to deepen that connection over time through their marketing strategies.

Realize people don't buy art because they need it, they buy because of connection. That connection might be with the artist, the process, the medium, the experience, the subject matter, or any combination of these factors, but there has to be a connection.

I've had the privilege since 2009 of making my living primarily from making and selling art to what many would call the luxury market. My clients are typically people who have multiple homes and enjoy purchasing and commissioning unique pieces of art for their homes ranging from several hundred to tens of thousands of dollars. Although many of them could probably afford anything they wanted, the price is almost never a part of the initial conversation, as they determine whether or not they want my work. For many artists, this begs the question: "If price is not really the main issue, then what DO they care about? What are they really looking for?"

Here are my top four things I know every art buyer is looking for:

- **Uniqueness**
  One of the first things I hear from people considering purchasing or commissioning my work is something like, "Wow, I've never seen anything like this before. I love it." Yes, it's beautiful, and there are a lot of beautiful things out there, but I'm also the only person that does what I do. Everything I create is a one of a kind, so there will never be another one exactly like it. I've said for years; differentiation is THE key to marketing. To think about it another way, just imagine what makes you and your work different in a field of 5, 10, 20, or 100 other artists who do essentially the same

thing you do. The more you develop a unique approach to your art making, the more buyers will be attracted to your work. Bottom line, they want something no one else has, because they can, and that's what makes it special.

- **Craftsmanship**
No matter how unique a piece of art is, people who can afford to invest $1,000, $2,000, $5,000 or more on a piece of art want to be sure that the piece is constructed with quality and craftsmanship. Are you using the best materials? Do you pay close attention to detail? Do you sweat the little things? At this level of selling, believe me, it matters. Your work should stand the test of time. Create pieces with longevity and legacy in mind, not just the quick sale.

- **Unparalleled Service**
The Biltmore Estate is here in Asheville, North Carolina where I live, and their staff is trained to practice something they've coined Gracious Hospitality. According to their website, through "being genuinely warm and authentically nice - we are able to deliver a customer experience that far outweighs the quality of any product we can sell." I've found that to be true in my own business as well. I always offer to deliver and install my work for free. I always carry new purchases to the car. I write thank-you notes. I drop by to visit clients and partners. Long story short, I just go the extra mile. People love it, and it's one of the hallmarks of buying a piece of art from me. I make it easy to do

business with me because it's a genuinely enjoyable experience.

- **Connection**

  One term many artists use is "collectors," as if these special art gods swoop down from the heavens, grace the doors of certain artists, and then swoop back into the ether. From what I've found over the years, people who buy lots of expensive, high-quality art are just people looking for connection. That connection might be with the artist, the subject matter, the artistic process, or even a special experience. Regardless, everyone loves to feel special and to genuinely connect in a way that's meaningful. This is especially true when it comes to people who purchase high-end art. Most people I encounter really enjoy the personal connection that commissioning a piece brings, including getting to know the artist, a personal studio visit, or a home visit to see their space and understand their preferences in interior design and art. This doesn't just happen in person either but online, too! Your website and social media should convey an authentic idea of who you are through your videos, images, and stories that will help deepen this connection over time with potential clients. Since connection points differ for each artist, you'll need to listen intently over time to understand why people connect with you and your work and then work diligently to deepen that connection over time.

Understanding and employing these four principles is core to the success of my business and any art business who wants to thrive over the long term.

"Do I have to be good at business to thrive as an artist?"

For most artists, business is our least favorite part of the equation, but alas, it's necessary for you to thrive financially. Think of your business as the vehicle that will take your art to the marketplace. Without that vehicle, what you have, my friend, is a hobby. You either create a working business or your art will stay a hobby. There is no other way around it.

Now, that being said, how your business functions is up to you. It doesn't mean that you have to do everything yourself. Yes, you need a website, an active social media presence, a legal business entity, and bookkeeping, but if you're not good at those, find someone to help you! A spouse, friend, or someone you could pay or barter with. Hiring a good local accountant and attorney to make sure you're set up and functioning properly with regards to licensing, corporate structure, and taxes might seem like a significant investment, but you're going to thank me if you listen to this advice! The enemy works in fear, and most of what people don't like about the business end of doing art is all based in fear. Expose the enemy! Get the help you need from professionals who can help you set things up correctly with growth in mind. Having those business elements is non-negotiable, but you don't necessarily have to be an expert in every area.

In my own business, I have found I have to give almost equal time to working both in the business and on the business. In the business means creating my art and being in the studio, interacting with clients, and selling art. You know, the part we all love. However, for my business vehicle to run, I also have to work ON the business doing things like marketing, business development, financial planning, and strategic partner interaction. For more on the business side of things, you can check out my book, *Crafting Your Brand*, and my Created to Thrive Mentoring program, where I go into detail on a variety of subjects, which are core for creating a thriving art business.

The bottom line is, you can't just let those things go and hope they will get done. To thrive financially, you'll have to develop some skills and resources in this area. Don't worry, as you actively pursue this area of growth in your life; God will be there with all the grace and resources you need!

"Is it okay to sell my art when God inspired me to create it?"

For artists who are believers in Jesus and want to honor Him with their gifting, this can be a very real question. You might wonder if it's okay to sell work that you feel was freely inspired by God. In short, the answer is a resounding "Yes!" However, not every artist is meant to sell his art, and herein lies the issue. It really depends on a few things, namely how an artist approaches his creative expression.

- **Art as Spiritual Experience**
  For most artists, the practice of art making is something that is innate. They can't imagine life without it. It's an extension of who they are, and when they are creating,

there's nothing else like it! There's an emotional release, a rush of pleasure, and feelings of overwhelming joy that are rarely found in any other experience. Many times, artists also make a deeper spiritual connection with God during this process. Either intentionally or unintentionally, artists might feel a real sense that they are not creating by themselves but are rather receiving inspiration from the Holy Spirit and creating with Him. Although this is not an experience unique to Christians, I believe the Father is releasing more of Himself, more of His Kingdom, and more of His nature to creatives who are taking the time to invite the Holy Spirit into the creative process.

When artists of all creative mediums enter into this process, it's an intimate place. Art making becomes a responsive act of worship where their ideas, tools, skills, and processes become yielded to the movement of the Holy Spirit within them. There's no faking it, because an artist knows when it's real. For many, there's no greater place of connection with the Father than when they are creating, whether it's writing a song, painting a picture, singing, dancing, weaving, or just dreaming. To downplay this experience would be a huge mistake because it's this process of connecting and creating that is so visceral and transforming for each artist. It's foundational to our experience and essential for our ongoing growth and connection with God.

In this place of art as spiritual experience, there doesn't have to be any rules or expectations. The experience of creating with God with no boundaries is all that matters. Whatever comes out comes out. It's all worship. It's all valid. It's all important to the artist's spiritual journey. The artist probably has a vocation that provides income for him and spends his 'free time' pursuing a creative outlet. There's never any pressure to sell or please anyone but himself and the Lord. For these artists, growth happens as a result of a nurtured relationship with God and the art-making process. There's no timetable or requirements on how or when that growth happens. It's art as worship, for the pleasure of creating, and that's enough.

- **Art as Ministry**
  It's rare that an artist creates in a vacuum without anyone knowing about his creative expression. For most creatives, we enjoy sharing our creativity with others, our friends, our family, even our faith community, and that only heightens the experience of creating. Nowadays, because of the rise of acceptance of art as a spiritual expression within the Church, many artists are finding they have the opportunity to share their art with others through doing things like art shows, painting on stage, performing on their worship team, or other wonderful expressions of creativity. This is an incredible opportunity for all creatives to take what's been happening in their private studio time with God and welcome others into that process. Instead of their art simply being a place of personal connection with God, now it also has the potential to become a vehicle for others to experience the transformative

Light of God through their art.

As with most things that involve other people, sometimes this can get a bit hairy. What do you do when someone doesn't understand or respond to your work in a way that's life-giving for you? How do you receive compliments? What if someone has a major encounter with the Lord through your work? It's never simple for an artist to put his creative expression out there for the public to interact with because it's not just about the work. It's bearing your soul and allowing others to come into your special place of connection with God. It's giving others the chance to judge your art and many times judge you as well. Depending on how you're wired, that can be exhilarating or a real emotional challenge.

Many artists now days are finding real acceptance within their faith communities as they create in the context of worship. People are inspired by their work, it heightens their own spiritual experience, and it allows them to create with others. It's these artists with whom we work the most with at The Worship Studio. They mostly create as worship and for the joy of the experience, have probably sold a few pieces here and there over the years but mostly enjoy giving their work away to others as a way to encourage them in their own spiritual journeys. Artists in this place often struggle with the concept of selling their work because they don't understand how they can or should sell something that's such a natural expression of their own heart and given to them by the Holy Spirit in the context of worship.

For artists who are creating for their own personal enjoyment and spiritual expression, I say, "Don't worry about selling your work." Allow it to be what it is: a joyful, creative, spiritual experience that you're sharing with others. Why put the pressure on yourself to sell or not sell if there's no specific calling to move into vocational art making? For many artists who are, for lack of a better word, hobbyists, the tension of feeling like they should sell their work causes more frustration than anything. In the end, it only impedes their creative process. I always encourage these folks to enjoy the process, freely give as you have freely received, and don't put undue pressure on yourself or your art.

- **Art as Vocation**
For most artists, especially Christians, who have moved into creating as their vocation, they still create from a place of spiritual experience and desire to connect with God through their own creative process. In fact, most, if not all, began in a place of creating simply as a response to their own inner need to create. I call it the compulsion to make, always searching for something to do with their hands. These artists still value the joy, spontaneity, and exhilaration of the creative process but at some point began to feel the desire to create as their vocation.

It might have been the result of a prophetic word, a

longstanding dream of theirs, the recognition that if they were going to keep doing this and getting better they needed to give their art more attention than they could as a hobby, or just because their work started selling and they followed God's favour on their work. However it happened, did this decision to create for money diminish their spiritual experience? Was God somehow displeased with them, because they were no longer just creating for the joy of creating? I believe the answer to these questions is a resounding "No!"

Remember, growth in the Kingdom is always based on stewardship of the gifts that people have been given, regardless of where they find themselves in culture. For artists, this most definitely includes their artistic gifting and their ability to hear, sense, feel, and receive from the Lord. Let me pause and say, however, that I don't believe becoming a full-time vocational artist means you've somehow achieved the ultimate maturity as an artist or as a Christian artist. Many of the best artists around choose to create as a hobby, for their personal enjoyment and have other vocations that they pursue to make their living. Many enjoy this because it allows them to come to their art making with no boundaries, requirements, or pressure. It's simply art for their personal enjoyment, sharing with others, and even worship.

Artists who have chosen to move into art making as their vocation, however, don't have the luxury of simply creating for personal enjoyment, although there is always joy that comes from the process. They have to consider the salability of their work, how it's marketed, priced, and presented to the public in a way that represents their values. Vocational artists can't give most of their work away because, for them, this is the primary way God has given them to make their financial provision. They have to think about things like dedicated studio space, gallery representation versus direct retail sales, inventory, shows, and marketing their work. These artists have to pay attention to who's buying their work, why, for what price, and to be used in what context, in order to continue to grow and thrive. To be successful, a vocational artist has to be both artist and entrepreneur. There is no either or if an artist is to be successful in the marketplace.

This is where a lot of Christians who are artists jump ship. They have this notion that artists who have chosen the vocational art path have somehow sold their soul to the art devil and have lost the essence of creating from a place of spiritual connection. How ridiculous! In my opinion, that's just a load of religious poppycock and emotional gobbledygook, and one of the biggest topics I address on a regular basis in my mentoring program, in addition to other really practical topics like pricing your artwork, developing strategic partnerships, finding your target market, and developing a clientele for your work.

Think about it. No one would think of making this accusation of artists being spiritual or artistic sellouts to someone who gets a million-dollar business idea from the Lord, yet somehow because we're creative, our motives and intentions are called into question. Should pastors not be paid because they receive inspiration from the Lord for their sermons and daily ministry?

Yes, being a vocational artist requires a different skill set and thought process, but it's no less spiritual for the artist who approaches his life and work as a Kingdom creative. Being a vocational Kingdom artist is a beautiful collaboration with God, in which the artist has the joyful opportunity to see and agree with Heaven, co-create their experience with the Holy Spirit, and enjoy the benefits of the Kingdom in their life while expecting transformation to be the result of their life and work. All along the way, they get to trust God completely for their provision, opportunities to sell their work, and new creative ideas.

I'm one of these vocational artists who did what I do creatively now as a hobby for 15 years before it became my primary income source. For me, this journey of becoming a full-time working artist has required so much more faith and connectedness with the Father than anything I've ever done. I have opportunities each and every day to listen, trust, and cooperate with the voice of the Holy Spirit, not only as I create art, but as I create a life and a business that God is using to bring finances into my family's life. I love the adventure of being a vocational artist and can't imagine doing anything else.

Enjoy Your Art

No matter where you are as an artist, creating for the love of the spiritual experience, doing it as a part of your ministry, or as a vocation, realize that God's joy over you is a simple fact that you're doing what He created you to do. As you grow and dream with Him, the ways you express and present your art will change. That's okay! Enjoy where you are now, and enjoy the growth process without putting undue pressure on yourself to be someone you're not. God has an incredible plan for your life and art, whether you sell it for thousands of dollars around the world, or offer it to Him as worship in the secret place. Just enjoy the Father, create with Him, and follow His lead.

Your Next Steps

If you're feeling inspired to step out on your journey as an artist from a hobbyist or emerging artist to becoming a thriving artist, then I want to invite you to become a part of my Created to Thrive Artist Mentoring Program. It's an online community of artists who are passionately pursuing their calling as artists in God's Kingdom, as I mentor them in their spiritual, artistic, and business development journey. The best part for me is helping artists like you discover the gold that's already living inside of them through the Kingdom!

Each week, I do a full-length teaching video on a variety of subjects important to growing artists, as well as a live question and answer session where you can ask me any question you have, and I answer it, live. All the video and written resources are archived in our members-only website at www.MattTommeyMentoring.com and within our members-only Facebook group.

The most special part of our community is the interaction between artists. Through our Facebook community, online and in-person events, life-changing relationships are being formed as we encourage each other along our creative journey.

This really can be your breakthrough year, and I'd love to help you take the next steps in seeing that actually happen. To find out more about the mentoring community, simply visit:

www.MattTommeyMentoring.com/artist-mentoring.html

and watch the video I have there. After that, if you're ready to become a part, you can do so right there on my website.

Thanks for the privilege of speaking into your creative journey! May God bless you abundantly as you pursue your creative calling in His Kingdom.

Free Resources

To bless you and better equip you at the beginning of your journey towards becoming the Kingdom Artist you were created to be, I've assembled a few essential resources that I want to make sure you have. These powerfully effective tools including, How to Make Money with Your Art, can be found at:

www.MattTommeyMentoring.com/cttfree

Other Books by Matt Tommey

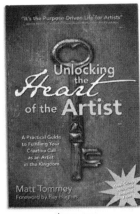

$14.99
Available in Print & Kindle

$14.99
Available in Print & Kindle

$14.99
Available in Print & Kindle

$14.99
Available in Print & Kindle

These books and other recommended resources are available at:
www.MattTommeyMentoring.com
and at other online retailers

Are You Ready to Thrive?

The Created to Thrive Experience Course is a dynamic community-based online course led by artist, author, and mentor Matt Tommey. Only available at select times, this six-week guided online journey picks up where the book ends to equip and encourage you to reach your full potential as a Kingdom Artist!

Enjoy 6 new challenging and powerful video messages from Matt while interacting with other Kingdom-minded artists from around the globe.

For More Information on this Life-Changing Course Visit:

www.MattTommeyMentoring.com
and look under the resources tab

Made in the USA
San Bernardino, CA
12 April 2018